Frommer's®

Lisbon
day BY day™

1st Edition

by Louise Pole-Baker

John Wiley & Sons, Ltd

Contents

UK Publisher: Sally Smith
Executive Project Editor: Daniel Mersey (Frommer's UK)
Commissioning Editor: Mark Henshall (Frommer's UK)
Development Editor: Tim Locke
Content Editor: Hannah Clement (Frommer's UK)
Cartographer: Tim Lohnes
Photo Research: Jill Emeny (Frommer's UK)

Wiley also publishes its books in a variety of electronic formats. Some content
that appears in print may not be available in electronic books.

British Library Cataloguing in Publication Data

A catalogue record for this book is available from the British Library

ISBN: 978-0-470-51976-9

Typeset by Wiley Indianapolis Composition Services

Printed and bound in China

5   4   3   2

A Note from the Publisher

Organizing your time. That's what this guide is all about.

Other guides give you long lists of things to see and do and then expect you to fit the pieces together. The Day by Day guides are different. These guides tell you the best of everything, and then they show you how to see it *in the smartest, most time-efficient way*. Our authors have designed detailed itineraries organized by time, neighborhood, or special interest. And each tour comes with a bulleted map that takes you from stop to stop.

Hoping to stroll through the Baixa, explore Lisbon's ancient heart, the Alfama, or enjoy a night of Portuguese food and fado? Planning a night out in Alcantra, or plotting a day of fun-filled activities with the kids? Whatever your interest or schedule, the Day by Days give you the smartest routes to follow. Not only do we take you to the top attractions, hotels, and restaurants, but we also help you access those special moments that locals get to experience— those "finds" that turn tourists into travelers.

The Day by Days are also your top choice if you're looking for one complete guide for all your travel needs. The best hotels and restaurants for every budget, the greatest shopping values, the wildest nightlife—it's all here.

Why should you trust our judgment? Because our authors personally visit each place they write about. They're an independent lot who say what they think and would never include places they wouldn't recommend to their best friends. They're also open to suggestions from readers. If you'd like to contact them, please send your comments my way at mspring@wiley.com, and I'll pass them on.

Enjoy your Day by Day guide—the most helpful travel companion you can buy. And have the trip of a lifetime.

Warm regards,

Michael Spring, Publisher
Frommer's Travel Guides

About the Author

Louise Pole-Baker, a freelance writer and editor, lives in Northern Ireland. She's written several guidebooks to Portugal and an online guide to Lisbon, the Algarve and Portugal for Whatsonwhen. Louise has an MA in Latin American Literature and culture.

Acknowledgments

Thank you to Carmo Botelho at the Lisbon Tourist Office for arranging access to numerous attractions and to staff at the Portuguese Tourist Office in London, particularly to Anne Morris for providing information and ideas. Thanks also to Frommer's Commissioning Editor, Mark Henshall, for his help and patience, to Editorial Assistant Jill Emeny for talking me through the photo selection and to my Development Editor, Tim Locke, for pulling everything into shape. I am also very grateful to Janet Barradas for introducing me to a few hidden gems and to my sister Teresa and family in Portugal for their tips. Above all, I would like to thank my husband, Sean Alexander McGrath, who took most of the photographs and gave invaluable support throughout.

Dedication

For my husband Sean.

An Additional Note

Please be advised that travel information is subject to change at any time—and this is especially true of prices. We therefore suggest that you write or call ahead for confirmation when making your travel plans. The authors, editors, and publisher cannot be held responsible for the experiences of readers while traveling. Your safety is important to us, however, so we encourage you to stay alert and be aware of your surroundings.

Star Ratings, Icons & Abbreviations

Every hotel, restaurant, and attraction listing in this guide has been ranked for quality, value, service, amenities, and special features using a **star-rating system.** Hotels, restaurants, attractions, shopping, and nightlife are rated on a scale of zero stars (recommended) to three stars (exceptional). In addition to the star-rating system, we also use a **kids icon** to point out the best bets for families. Within each tour, we recommend cafes, bars, or restaurants where you can take a break. Each of these stops appears in a shaded box marked with a coffee-cup-shaped bullet ☕.

The following **abbreviations** are used for credit cards:

AE	American Express	DISC	Discover	V	Visa
DC	Diners Club	MC	MasterCard		

Frommers.com

Now that you have this guidebook to help you plan a great trip, visit our website at **www.frommers.com** for additional travel information on more than 3,500 destinations. We update features regularly to give you instant access to the most current trip-planning information available. At Frommers. com, you'll find scoops on the best airfares, lodging rates, and car rental bargains. You can even book your travel online through our reliable travel booking partners.

A Note on Prices

In the "Take a Break" and "Best Bets" sections of this book, we have used a system of dollar signs to show a range of costs for 1 night in a hotel (the price of a double-occupancy room) or the cost of an entrée (main meal) at a restaurant. Use the following table to decipher the dollar signs:

Cost	Hotels	Restaurants
$	under $100	under $10
$$	$100–$200	$10–$20
$$$	$200–$300	$20–$30
$$$$	$300–$400	$30–$40
$$$$$	over $400	over $40

An Invitation to the Reader

In researching this book, we discovered many wonderful places—hotels, restaurants, shops, and more. We're sure you'll find others. Please tell us about them, so we can share the information with your fellow travelers in upcoming editions. If you were disappointed with a recommendation, we'd love to know that, too. Please write to:

Frommer's Lisbon Day by Day, 1st Edition
Wiley Publishing, Inc. • 111 River St. • Hoboken, NJ 07030-5774

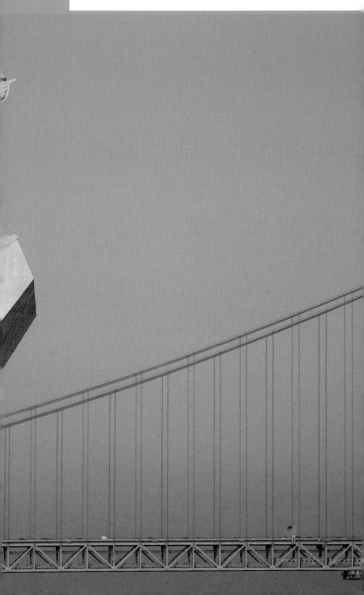

10 Favorite
Moments

10 Favorite Moments

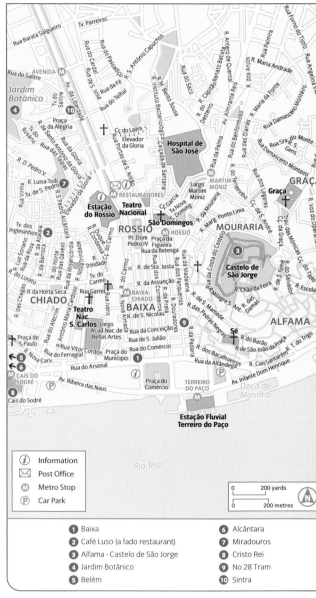

Legend:

- *(i)* Information
- ✉ Post Office
- Ⓜ Metro Stop
- Ⓟ Car Park

0 — 200 yards
0 — 200 metres

① Baixa
② Café Luso (a fado restaurant)
③ Alfama - Castelo de São Jorge
④ Jardim Botânico
⑤ Belém
⑥ Alcântara
⑦ Miradouros
⑧ Cristo Rei
⑨ No 28 Tram
⑩ Sintra

In the past 20 years Lisbon has opened its doors to the world. I love this place for its history and culture, from its glorious seafarers to melancholy fado music and literary masters – but it's by no means stagnated in the past. Since Portugal joined the E.U. in 1986, the city has built bridges into the future, from the modern Parque das Nações to the revamped Alcântara docks. It all adds up to an exhilarating cocktail of art and architecture, vibrant street life and café culture, traditional eateries and hip bars.

1 Strolling through the Baixa. At the center of historic Lisbon, the grid of neo-classical streets known as the Baixa is the easiest place to get your bearings. Start in the airy Praça de Comércio, a meeting point for visitors and *Lisboetas*, and drift through the monumental Arco Triunfal archway into the bustling Rua Augusta, where streetsellers tout souvenirs and paintings. *See p 64.*

2 A night of Portuguese food and *fado*. When it comes to food and entertainment, the Portuguese know how to put on a good spread. I like to sample the best *bacalhau* (salt cod) dishes, skewers of meat and fresh fish at a *fado* restaurant in the Bairro Alto or at one of many small, tile-covered restaurants in the heart of the Alfama. *See p 101.*

3 Exploring the Alfama. The Alfama is Lisbon's ancient heart, a

Torre de Belém and the River Tejo.

tangle of cobbled streets and narrow steps. Start by the turrets of the Castelo de São Jorge (St. George's Castle), taking in the panoramic city views before following the tram tracks down past the Sé (cathedral) (see p 58). I make a point of rising early on Tuesdays or Saturdays for the *Feira da Ladra* (Thieves Market) here, a treasure trove of bric-à-brac and painted ceramics. *See p 84.*

4 Cooling off in the Botanic Gardens. I know of no better haven from the summer heat than these lush gardens, between the Bairro Alto and Rato. Stroll along under the shade of tall palms, breathing in the scents of orchids and listening to water trickle into the ponds—the

The Arco Triunfal leads through to the busy Rua Augusta.

city traffic is just a faint buzz. *See p 95.*

5 The Manueline architecture of Belém. The Mosteiro dos Jerónimos (Jerónimos Monastery) and Torre de Belém (Belém Tower) are the pinnacles of Portuguese architecture. These structures are full of clues—such as carved ropes and sculptures of monarchs—reflecting Portugal's Golden Age of Discovery, when its seafarers stepped out on a voyage of exploration that changed the world. *See p 28.*

6 A night out in Alcântara. The old warehouses of the Alcântara docks have been transformed into one of the city's most popular nightspots. Take in the river views from the terraces of its buzzing cafés and bars, and enjoy some of the best in innovative Portuguese cuisine. *See p 115.*

7 Taking in the city views from Lisbon's *miradouros*. I never tire of Lisbon's hills: the rewards are the views from the *miradouros* (viewing points). Discover your favorites: mine include the Castelo de São Jorge, looking towards the ruined

Looking up at the Cristo Rei statue.

Convento do Carmo; São Pedro de Alcântara, for an Alfama panorama; and the top of Parque Eduardo VII, which looks down its formal gardens and the tree-lined Avenida da Liberdade. *See Castelo de São Jorge, p 8.*

8 Stand at the summit of the Cristo Rei statue. Take a ferry across the Tagus River to visit the Cristo Rei statue, which stands arms open-wide majestically in Almada. Ride the elevator to the top for a heady sight of the 25 de Abril Bridge below and panoramic views of the city. *See p 43.*

9 Riding the No. 28 Tram. Whether your feet can take the cobbled hills or not, this is still a great way to see Lisbon's oldest districts. The old red tram creaks and trundles up and down the hills from the Alfama through the Baixa to the Bairro Alto and on to Estrela and Campo Ourique. *See p 7.*

10 Immersing yourself in Sintra's fantasy. I side with Lord Byron's description of Sintra's royal palaces and their mountain setting as a "Glorious Eden". There are two main palaces: one in the town, the other a romantic creation on a hilltop,

Palácio Nacional da Pena in Sintra.

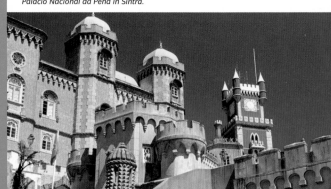

1 The Best Full-Day Tours

The Best **in One Day**

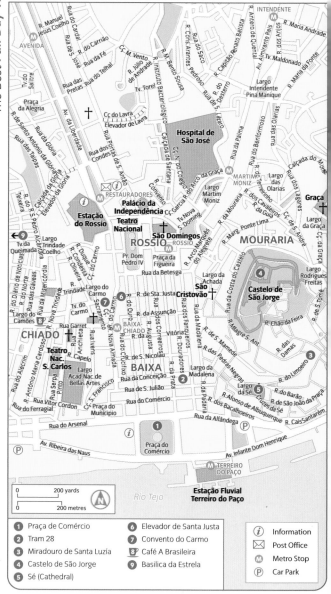

| 0 | 200 yards |
| 0 | 200 metres |

❶ Praça de Comércio		❻ Elevador de Santa Justa	
❷ Tram 28		❼ Convento do Carmo	
❸ Miradouro de Santa Luzia		❽ Café A Brasileira	
❹ Castelo de São Jorge		❾ Basilica da Estrela	
❺ Sé (Cathedral)			

ⓘ	Information
✉	Post Office
Ⓜ	Metro Stop
Ⓟ	Car Park

This full-day tour gives you a rich and concise introduction to Lisbon's historic center and avoids traveling any great distance. It follows part of the route of the No. 28 tram, the most celebrated of Lisbon's rickety old trams. Start early to beat the crowds and take in the individual districts of Alfama, Baixa, Chiado, Bairro Alto, and Estrela. **START Praça de Comércio. Metro: Baixa/Chiado. Tram: 12, 15. Bus: 2, 81, 92, 711, 713.**

1 ★★ Praça de Comércio. This stately neo-classical square (praça) is open to the river Tagus (Rio Tejo) on one side, with the grid of streets that make up the Baixa Pombalina on the inland side. Note the 18th-century bronze statue at the center of the square. This is Dom José I (1714–77), king at the time of Lisbon's great earthquake, although it was the Marquês de Pombal who rebuilt the city in the 18th century. The square is usually my first port of call where I pick up information and tourist discount cards from the Lisbon Welcome Center. Several sightseeing tour buses, trams, and buses also stop here. The Arco Triunfal (Triumph Arch) marks the entrance to the Baixa's pedestrian street, Rua de Augusta, which buzzes with street sellers, artists, and tourists. ⏱ 20 min. Metro: Baixa-Chiado. Tram: 15, 18, 25. Bus: 2, 81, 92, 711, 713.

2 ★★★ kids Tram 28. I regularly use this tram, a popular route with tourists as it links several of the city's historic districts. Although Lisbon is generally a safe city, the tram is renowned for pickpockets. Don't let that spoil your enjoyment: just keep valuables tucked away and enjoy the novel ride as the tram clanks along the cobbled streets. ⏱ 10 min. Eastbound Mon–Fri 6.20am–11.20pm, Sat 6.15am–11.05pm, Sun 7.25am–11.05pm. Westbound Mon–Fri 5.40am–11.10pm, Sat 5.45am–10.35pm, Sun 6.45am–10.35pm. Services every few minutes. 1.30€ single.

3 ★ Miradouro de Santa Luzia. One of the city's most famous miradouros (viewing points), this looks over the steep Alfama district and down towards the Tagus. I like to stop and linger over a coffee

Praça de Comércio, a great place to start your tour.

Tram 28, which links several of the city's historic districts.

taking in the views. It's also located by the access road up to the castle. Stop at the small Igreja de Santa Luzia, a church (*igreja*) run by the Order of Malta. In the square at the front, there's a tile panel with a city panorama. 🕐 *20 min. (with coffee). Tram: 12, 28. Bus: 37.*

④ ★★★ Castelo de São Jorge. The arch marks the entrance to this castle, but buy your tickets at the Casa do Gobernador (Governor's House). Head directly through the barriers into the leafy square, Praça das Armas with its mighty statue of Dom Afonso Henriques (1109–85), Portugal's first king and liberator from Moorish rule.

Built in or around the 10th century by the Moors as a means of defense, the castle was extended as a Royal Palace from the 13th to 16th centuries, but fell into neglect after the royal family moved to what is now the Praça de Comércio. Very little of the original structure remains, but 20th-century reconstruction evokes something of what it was. The large leafy square offers spectacular city views, and the inner courtyard of the castle often echoes to the sounds of musicians playing, as you climb the towers. 🕐 *60–90 min. Alfama.* ☎ *21-880-0620. www. castelosaojorge.egeac.pt. Admission 5€, 30% discount Lisboa Card, free under 10s & seniors. Open Nov–Feb 9am–6pm; Mar–Oct 9am–9pm.*

⑤ ★ Sé (Cathedral). I like to follow the tram tracks downhill on foot to take in the atmosphere of the Alfama district. Built on the site of an old mosque in the 12th century, the cathedral has also been added to over time. Although it can seem austere inside, it has certain details I find particularly appealing, such as the decorated capitals of the main portal, with carved figures of the Archangel Michael and fighting men mounted on strange beasts, and the vaulted ceilings of the main nave and ambulatory. Also, seek out the impressive Gothic tombs and cloisters with double arches. 🕐 *20–45 min. Largo da Sé.* ☎ *21-886-6752. Admission free; cloisters 2.50€. Open daily 9am–7pm; cloisters Oct–Apr only, Mon–Sat 10am–6pm, Sun 2–6pm. Tram: 12, 28. Bus: 37.*

⑥ ★★ Elevador de Santa Justa. The tram track trundles back down into the heart of the Baixa, kinder on the feet than the cobbled hills of the Alfama. At the western end of Rua Santa Justa is the eye-catching iron Santa Justa elevator, built by engineer Raoul Mesnier du Ponsard in 1898–1901, to transport people to the streets above (it still works). At the top there's a café with great views of the Baixa, Rossio Square, and the Castle. 🕐 *10–30 min. Rua de Santa Justa. Admission 1.30€ or free with Carris travel pass; Open winter daily 7am–9pm;*

summer Mon–Sat 7am–11pm; Sun &
public holidays 9am–11pm. Metro:
Baixa-Chiado, Rossio. Tram: 15, 28.
Bus: 2, 9, 36, 37, 44, 81, 92.

⑦ ★★★ **Convento do Carmo
& Museu Arqueológico.** The
convent, originally dating back to
the 14th century, stands as an eerily
majestic monument to the 1755
earthquake. Once inside the roof-
less ruins tower above like the
bones of a huge dinosaur. There is
a wealth of archeological exhibits,
including ancient Jewish grave-
stones, an Egyptian sarcophagus
and baroque tiled panels, but its
contemplative air is what grabs me:
sit on the steps and take in the
whole scene. 🕑 *45 min.–1 hr. Largo
do Carmo, 4.* ☎ *21-346-0473.
Admission 2.50€, 1.50€ students &
seniors; free under 14s & public holidays until 2pm.*

*The towering skeleton of Convento do
Carmo destroyed in the 1755 earthquake.*

⑧ ★★ **A Brasileira.** Stop for a coffee and snack at this café, once frequented by modernist poet Fernando
Pessoa (1888–1935). You'll know
when you're there as there's a bronze
statue of him sitting outside. *Rua Garrett, 120.* ☎ *21-834-6. Tram: 28.*

⑨ ★★ **Basílica da Estrela.**
Tram 28 stops directly outside this
basilica, built shortly after the earthquake, in 1779, by the queen Dona
Maria I (1734–1816), who is
entombed here. The two white bell
towers and dome make it one of Lisbon's great landmarks, with the figures above the four columns of the
façade representing faith, adoration,
liberty, and gratitude. Inside the
church is a combination of pink,
black, and white marble and paintings by Italian masters. 🕑 *30 min.–
1 hr. Largo da Estrela.* ☎ *21-396-
0915. Open Tues–Sat 7.30am–1pm &
3–8pm; Sun 8am–2pm & 3–8pm.*

Castelo de São Jorge's internal walls were mostly rebuilt in the 20th century.

The Best **in Two Days**

1. Museu Nacional de Arte Antiga
2. Antiga Confeitaria de Belém
3. Mosteiro dos Jerónimos
4. Museu Nacional de Arqueologia
5. Museu da Marinha
6. Cafe Quadrante
7. Centro Cultural de Belém
8. Torre de Belém
9. Padrão dos Descobrimentos

This tour leads you to some of Lisbon's most iconic sights, venturing out of the city center and west along the Tagus in Belém. Start early to enjoy a couple of hours in the Museu Nacional de Arte Antiga on the way, taking the rest of the day to explore Belém. Note you'll need to take a bus or tram to Belém: it's too far to walk. **START Museu Nacional de Arte Antiga. Tram: 15, 18, 25. Bus: 6, 28, 60, 713, 714, 727, 794.**

① ★ **Museu Nacional de Arte Antiga (MNAC).** You'll need to allocate plenty of time to do justice to Portugal's most valuable art collection, housed in a 17th-century palace (with an extension on the site of an older Carmelite convent). You can see the entire collection in a brisk couple of hours, or make a bee-line for the prized collection of Portuguese religious paintings and sculpture from the 15th and 16th centuries. Also seek out the baroque chapel on the first floor, the only part of the convent that still remains. If you've time to spare, take in the varied displays of jewelry, ceramics, and furniture from France, Portugal, and former colonies. ⏱ *60 min. Rua das Janelas Verdes.* ☎ *21-391-2800. www.mnarteantiga-ipmuseus.pt. Admission 3€, 60% discount youth card holders, 50% discount 15–25 years & seniors, free under 14s and on Sun and public holidays. Open Tues 2–6pm, Wed–Sun 10am–6pm. Tram: 15, 28. Bus: 6, 28, 60, 713, 714, 727, 794.*

The Golden Age of Discovery

Portugal's most prominent period of maritime exploration took place during the 15th and 16th centuries, with the aim of finding new trade and Christianizing the Muslims to the south. The Infante Dom Henrique, better known as Henry the Navigator (1394–1460), led the first push beginning with his expedition to the Moroccan city of Céuta in 1415. Further explorations sailed south along the west African coast, and in 1487 Bartolomeu Dias (1450–1500) made it round the Cape of Good Hope. A little over a decade later, Vasco da Gama (1460–1524) crossed the Indian Ocean, bypassing the arduous overland Silk Road and fueling the spice trade. In 1500 Pedro Alvares Cabral "discovered" Brazil, and in 1519 Fernão de Magalhães (1480–1521) set out to find a western route to the Indonesian spice islands. Funded by the Spanish, he is better known as Ferdinand Magellan. He reached the Philippines but died there in 1521.

2 Antiga Confeitaria de Belém. When you alight from the tram, cross the road to this café, recognizable for its blue canopies. Stand at the counter for a quick coffee and one of their famous delicious *pasteis de Belém* (custard tarts), or slip into one of the tiled back rooms for waiter service. *Rua de Belém, 84-92.* ☎ *21-363-7423. Tram: 15.*

3 ★★★ Mosteiro dos Jerónimos. A national icon, this monastery constantly strikes me for its size and delicate carved details. Built on the orders of Dom Manuel I, in the 16th century, it is considered one of the most important examples of Manueline architecture (see p 28). To avoid the crowds, come in late afternoon or out of season.

16th-century Mosteiro dos Jerónimos.

Mosteiro dos Jerónimos

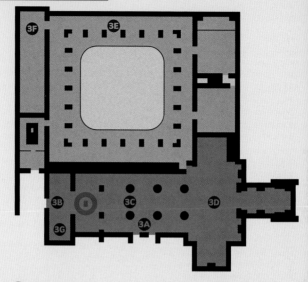

The **3A** **south portal** is the visual centerpiece of the exterior, with elaborate carvings of the Virgin of Belém (Bethlehem) surrounded by angels, rich floral details, and scenes from the life of São Jerónimo. At the **3B** **main portal**, look out for the intricate figurines of Dom Manuel I and his queen, Dona Maria, and scenes from the birth of Christ.

Inside, the **3C** **church** has three naves, and the ornate tombs of writers Fernando Pessoa (1888–1935) and Luis de Camões (1524–80). The main nave's vaulted ceiling is supported by just six columns, entwined with characteristic Manueline carved ropes and exotic flora (see p 24). At the far end is the **3D** **capela-mor**, the main chapel, built for (the queen) Dona Catarina in 1571 with panels of Mannerist paintings.

For me the **3E** **cloisters and refectory** are the real highlights, the cloisters a showcase of Manueline carvings. The best feature of the **3F** **refectory** are the *azulejos* (tiled) panels along the walls, added in the 17th century. Upstairs in the **choir 3G**, you can take in the church from above and admire the carved choir stalls. ⏱ *30–60 min. Praça do Império.* ☎ *21-362-0034. www.mosteirojeronimos.pt. Admission cloisters 4.50€, 2.25€ kids 4–15 & seniors, 1.80€ youth card holders, free under 14s, general public Sun & public holidays until 2pm. Open Oct–Apr Tues–Sun 10am–5pm; May–Sep Tues–Sun 10am–6.30pm. Train: Belém. Tram: 15. Bus: 27, 28, 29, 43, 49, 51.*

4 ★★ Museu Nacional de Arqueologia. You can either enter this archeology museum through the door opposite the main portal of the church or through the main entrance at the front of the building. Often ignored by visitors who dash off to lunch after seeing the church and cloisters, there are various treasures here dating from the Paleolithic to medieval periods. Highlights include some near-complete Roman mosaics as well as entrancing and elaborate Egyptian funerary masks. ⏱ *45–60 min. Praça do Império.* ☎ *21-362-0000. www.mn arqueologia-ipmuseus.pt. Admission 3€, 1.50€ 15–25 years, students & seniors, 2.25€ Lisboa Card; free under 14s, Lisboa Card, general public Sun 10am–2pm. Open Tues–Sun 10am–6pm. Train: Belém. Tram: 15. Bus 27, 28, 29, 43, 49, 51, 112..*

5 ★ Museu da Marinha. At the far end of the former monastery, the Maritime Museum is the place to learn about Portugal's momentous relationship with the sea. From a typical Manueline vaulted entrance hall, you are introduced to the first explorers and then taken on a journey through seafaring history, including the Golden Age of Discovery as well as naval ships, merchant sailing, fishing, and royal vessels. There's information in English en route, but if time's limited, head for the highlights: objects from the Far East, such as porcelain and frightening Samurai swords; and the Pavilhão das Galeotas, a large pavilion with life-size models of royal boats, fishing and other craft. ⏱ *45–60 min. Praça do Império.* ☎ *21-362-0019. Admission 3€, 1.50€ kids 6–17, students & seniors, 2.25€ Lisboa Card, free under 6s & general public Sun 10am–1pm. Open Oct–Mar Tues–Sun 10am–5pm; Apr–Sep Tue–Sun 10am–6pm. Train: Belém. Tram: 15. Bus: 27, 28, 29, 43, 49, 51, 112.*

6 ★ Café Quadrante. A useful budget option for a quick lunch, inside the Belém Cultural Center. It's self-service and offers healthy eating options as well as hot international dishes. *Avenida de Brasília.* ☎ *21-362-0865. Centro Cultural de Belém, Praça do Imperio.* ☎ *21-362-9256. $.*

The ornate south portal of of Mosteiro dos Jerónimos.

⑦ ★★★ Centro Cultural de Belém. The Belém Cultural Center's sleek, modern form is not to everyone's taste, but that's part of what I like about it. To me it's a monumental and forward-looking statement that respects the older constructions around it. This has become one of the most vibrant cultural centers in the country for contemporary music and the performing arts (see p 129). Completed in 1992, it hosts temporary exhibitions by renowned modern artists and, from 2007, has been the permanent home of the **Museu Berardo, Colecção de Arte Moderno e Contemporâneo**. The permanent collection of this contemporary and modern art museum is displayed on rotation by art movement or theme, from Surrealism to Pop Art and Postmodernism (see p 48). The café and restaurant are great for lunch: clean and reasonable, there's a buffet service and balconies overlooking Belém and the river. There's also a well-stocked wine store and a Bertrand bookshop with art books. ⏱ *30–60 min. Praça do Império.* ☎ *21-361-2400. www.ccb. pt. www.museubardo.com. Admission*

free at time of writing; phone to check prices. Open (museum) daily 10am–7pm (Fri until 10pm). Train: Belém. Tram: 15. Bus: 27, 28, 29, 43, 49, 51, 112.

⑧ ★★★ kids Torre de Belém. Along with the Mosteiro dos Jerónimos, the Belém Tower is a UNESCO World Heritage Site and another superb example of Manueline architecture. Built in the 16th century to defend the city, the monument looks out along the river to the sea. It stands out on its own but despite the walk along the busy Avenida de Brasília, it's a relaxing place with a shaded park leading to benches on the waterfront. Take in the castellated tower from the outside with carvings of ropes, regal domes, shields, and intricate balconettes with the cross of the Knights of Christ. You can see along the river from the balcony but climb the steps to the top of the tower for more impressive views and intriguing close-ups of carved coats of arms, flora, and animal heads. ⏱ *30–45 min. Avenida de Brasília.* ☎ *21-362-0034. Admission 3€, 1.50€ kids 4–15 & seniors, 1.20€*

The vibrant Centro Cultural de Belém.

youth card holders; free under 14s & general public Sun &d public holidays until 2pm. Open Oct–Apr Tue–Sun 10am–5pm; May–Sep Tue–Sun 10am–6.30pm. Train: Belém. Tram: 15. Bus: 27, 28, 29, 43, 49, 51, 112.

⑨ ★★★ Padrão dos Descobrimentos. The 50m-high Discoveries Monument is an aptly shaped homage to Portugal's Golden Age of Discovery and a great place to end your day's tour. First built in 1940 by architect José Cotinelli Telmo and sculptor Leopoldo de Almeida as part of the Portuguese World Exhibition, it was reconstructed in concrete in 1960 to mark the fifth centenary of Henry the Navigator's death. From the side you can see it represents a *caravela* (Portuguese explorers' boat) and from the bow to the stern, it is lined with major figures of the Discoveries, from Henry the Navigator and Vasco da Gama to Luis Vaz de Camões and Nuno Gonçalves. You have to pay to go inside where there's a viewing platform and exhibitions, but you can see the outside for free any time. ⏱ *20 min. Avenida de Brasília.* ☎ *21-303-1950. www.padrao descobrimentos. egeac.pt. Admission to viewing platform and exhibitions 2.50€, 1.50€ kids 7–8, students under 25, seniors, 30% discount Lisboa Card. Open*

Torre de Belém, a welcome sight for mariners.

Oct–Apr Tue–Sun 10am–6pm; May–Sep Tue–Sun 10am–7pm. Train: Belém. Tram: 15. Bus: 27, 28, 29, 43, 49, 51, 112.

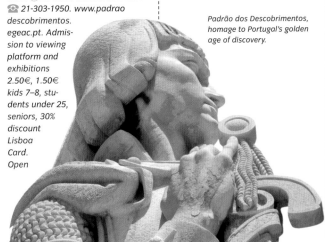

Padrão dos Descobrimentos, homage to Portugal's golden age of discovery.

The Best **in Three Days**

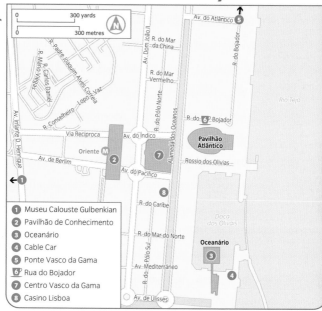

0 — 300 yards
0 — 300 metres

1. Museu Calouste Gulbenkian
2. Pavilhão de Conhecimento
3. Oceanário
4. Cable Car
5. Ponte Vasco da Gama
6. Rua do Bojador
7. Centro Vasco da Gama
8. Casino Lisboa

During the first two days you would have seen some of Lisbon's most iconic attractions, but with an extra day you have the chance to spend time at the eclectic Gulbenkian Museum and Garden, visit the city's modern district of Parque das Nações, and finish with a spot of shopping and maybe some entertainment. START **Praça de Comércio. Metro Baixa-Chiado. Tram: 12, 15. Bus: 2, 81, 92, 711, 713.**

1 ★★★ **Museu Calouste Gulbenkian.** The eclectic collection at the Gulbenkian Museum is a treasure trove of art brought together by Calouste Sarkis Gulbenkian, after whom the museum is named (see below). You could spend all morning here so make an early start and plan your visit; choose from the Oriental and Classical Art collection or European Art or cherry-pick from each section. I've done both in one day but would advise making your choice from the highlights. These include the Eastern Islamic Art, which is particularly outstanding because this was Gulbenkian's special passion, along with the paintings and sculptures by European masters (see p 49). If you have time, relax outside for 10 minutes in the gardens, which are a lush mix of greenery, water features, and some superb sculptures. ⏱ 1–3 hr. *Avenida de Berna, 45A.* ☎ *21-782-3000. www.museu.gulbenkian.pt. Admission 4€, 20% discount Lisboa Card; 50% discount seniors &*

students, free under 12s. Open Tue–Sun 10am–5.45pm. Metro: São Sebastião, Praça de Espanha. Bus: 16, 26, 31, 46, 56.

② **Pavilhão de Conhecimento.** The Knowledge Pavilion is one for the kids, an interactive science and knowledge centre with fun challenges aimed at different ages. The exhibits introduce children to everything from the natural elements to our own abilities and senses. *Alameda dos Oceanos; ☎ 21 891 7100. www.pavconhecimento.pt. Admission 6€, 3€ seniors; 7–17 yrs 2.50€. 3–6 yrs; free under 3 yrs; 13€ families (1 or 2 adults with children up to 17 years). Tue–Fri 10am–6pm; weekends and bank holidays 11am–7pm. Metro & Trains Oriente; Bus 5, 10, 19, 21, 28, 50 ,68, 81, 82, 85.*

③ ★★★ **kids** **Oceanário.** The Oceanarium is one of the most expensive attractions in the city, but definitely worth the entrance fee. You follow the arrows through four biospheres, first above water and then below. Between each habitat is the Global Ocean where you'll come face to face with sharks, groupers, graceful stingray, and the big (but hardly graceful), one-ton sun fish.

Museu Calouste Gulbenkian across its lush gardens..

Each of the four habitats has the temperature, lighting, flora and fauna of its geographic region, so in the North Atlantic you'll see puffins and razorbills above water and anemones, jellyfish, rocky reefs and sea grass beds below. Look out for the penguins and seals in the icy Antarctic, the cute sea otters in the Temperate Pacific, and the colorful birds and sea urchins in the Tropical Indian. *⏱ 60–90 min. Doca dos Olivais. ☎ 21-891-7002. www.oceanario.pt. Admission 10.50€, 5.75€ seniors; 5€ kids 4–12, free under 3s. Open*

Calouste Sarkis Gulbenkian (1869–1955)

Born in Istanbul to a wealthy Armenian merchant family, Gulbenkian studied in Marseilles and London before making his own fortune in gasoline. He became an avid art collector, accumulating a large number of Islamic objects as well as painting, sculpture, and decorative art by European masters. He came to Lisbon during World War Two and there he found peace, staying until his death in 1955. He donated a number of important works to the Museu Nacional de Arte Antiga from 1949–52, and in his will he requested the creation of a foundation in his name with the aim of displaying his huge collection of art.

Parque das Nações: an overview

Built for Expo '98, Nations' Park is an ultra-modern district. It might not be to everyone's taste, but you have everything you need in one place. The clean, open feel, and relaxed pace bring me back here. I love everything from the Discoveries theme of the tiled panels in the **metro station** and the palm-tree effect of the **Oriente train station** to the curious scattering of sculptures, and the **Portuguese Pavilion**, its curved roof a masterpiece of architecture and engineering. Then there are the spectacular views of the **Vasco da Gama Bridge**. I'll happily wander on foot from one end to the other but there's also a **tourist train**, a **bike hire facility** by the Oceanarium, and a **cable car**. With little traffic, plenty of family-friendly eateries (see p 101) and attractions, the park is perfect for kids. You can buy a tourist card from the park's information desk (15.50€, 8.50€ kids 4–12), which gives you free entry to the Oceanário, Pavilhão de Conhecimento, cable car, and tourist train, with discounts on bike hire and at some restaurants. *Parque das Nações. www.parquedasnacoes.pt. Metro: Vasco da Gama. Bus: 5, 25, 28, 44, 708, 750, 759, 794.*

Apr–Oct daily 10am–7pm, Nov–Mar daily 10am–6pm, 25 Dec 1pm–6pm, New Year's Day 12pm–6pm. Metro & Train: Oriente. Bus: 5, 25, 28, 44, 708, 750, 759, 794.

4 ★ kids **Cable Car.** If you don't mind heights (and the occasional wobble during windy weather), then hop on the cable car for a bird's-eye view. Starting south of the Oceanarium, you'll appreciate the vast width of the river on one side and look across the Pavilhão Atlântico, exhibition center, and restaurants below you on the left. Unless you're not a big walker, just buy a single ticket and take time to have lunch or a drink at the dozens of

restaurants on the way back to the metro. ⏱ *10–15 min. Between Doca dos Olivais and Torre de Vasco da Gama.* ☎ *21-895-6143. www.parquedasnacoes.pt. Admission 3.50€ one way, 5.50€ round trip, 1.80€ kids 5–14 & seniors one way, 3€ kids 5–14 & seniors round trip, free under 5s. Open Oct–May Mon–Fri 11am–7pm; Sat, Sun and public holidays 10am–8pm; Jun–Sep Mon–Fri 11am–8pm; Sat, Sun and public holidays 10am–9pm. Metro & Train: Oriente. Bus: 5, 25, 28, 44, 708, 750, 759, 794.*

5 ★ **Ponte Vasco da Gama.** The Vasco da Gama Bridge Opened in

Oceanario's mascot

1998, in time for Expo '98, it is the longest bridge in Europe, measuring an impressive 17.2km, around 12km of which cross the Tagus. To me it represents a connection between the city's past and future. Named after one of its most famous explorers, the bridge crosses the water in a new direction, providing pan-European trade routes. ⏱ *5 mins.* *Metro: Oriente; 5, 25, 28, 44, 708, 750, 759, 794.*

Oriente Train Station

6 **Rua do Bojador.** More of a strip than a street, this is a long line of restaurants beside Lisbon's exhibition center, FIL, and facing the Garcia Horta gardens and the river beyond. I'm impressed by the wide choice on offer here, from traditional Portuguese and specialist fish restaurants to Spanish tapas, Italian, Irish, and more. Many have terraces outside for eating al fresco and others transform from family restaurants to discos and karaoke clubs. There's also something for all budgets but none of these are likely to break the bank. *$–$$$.*

7 **Centro Vasco da Gama.** Large, light and clean, this convenient indoor shopping center has train and metro lines below and, in usual Portuguese style, a varied selection of eateries. There's everything here from high-street fashion favorites to trendy household items, and a supermarket where you can buy some typical Portuguese goodies to take home. There's also a multiplex moviehouse showing all the latest blockbuster films in English with Portuguese subtitles, so restless kids should be well entertained

A comfortable way to explore the ultra-modern Parque das Nações.

Outdoor Art in Parque das Nações

One of the things I love about the Nations' Park is the attention to detail. Scattered around are works of art inspired by myths and legends, each one bringing the district to life. Two iron sculptures are among the most striking, and my own personal favorites: Rhizome by Antony Gormley (outside the Portuguese Pavilion) is a collection of legs and torsos balanced in an impossible acrobatic pose, and Homem—Sol by Jorge Viera opposite the Vasco da Gama shopping center is a spiky metal cactus, almost human in form. Also see the Rio Vivo, a three-part mosaic inspired by fish, in Passeio Neptuno made from Italian tesserae by Rolando Sá Nogueira, and Pedro Proença's Portuguese stone pavement in Cais dos Argonautos depicting Monstros Marinhos, marine monsters as they were imagined in the Middle Ages.

and watered here. ⏲ *30min.–2 hr. Avenida João II.* ☎ *21-893-0601. www.centrovascodagama.pt. Open daily 10am–12am. Metro & Train: Oriente. Bus: 5, 25, 28, 44, 708, 750, 759, 794.*

❽ **Casino Lisboa.** This is a fairly recent addition to the Nations' Park. A large, sleek black and mirrored

building, the casino offers gaming (slots, blackjack, poker, and more), glamorous shows by international performers, restaurants and bars. ⏲ *30min. plus. Alameda dos Oceanos. www.casinolisboa.pt. Open Sun–Thu 3pm–3am, Fri, Sat and public holiday evenings 4pm–4am. Metro: Oriente. Bus: 5, 25, 28, 44, 708, 750, 759, 794.* ●

Vasco da Gama shopping center.

2 The Best Special-Interest Tours

Grand Designs

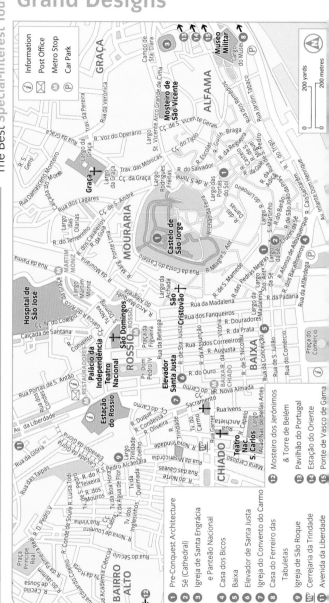

Legend:
- ⓘ Information
- ✉ Post Office
- Ⓜ Metro Stop
- Ⓟ Car Park

Ⓐ

0 — 200 yards
0 — 200 metres

Map labels:
GRAÇA · ALFAMA · MOURARIA · MARTIM MONIZ · ROSSIO · BAIXA · CHIADO · BAIRRO ALTO

Mosteiro de São Vicente · Castelo de São Jorge · Museu Militar · Graça · São Domingos · São Cristóvão · Hospital de São José · Palácio da Independência · Teatro Nacional · Estação do Rossio · Elevador Santa Justa · Teatro Nac. S. Carlos · Praça do Comércio

Tour list:
1. Pre-Conquest Architecture
2. Sé (Cathedral)
3. Igreja de Santa Engrácia e Panteão Nacional
4. Casa dos Bicos
5. Baixa
6. Elevador de Santa Justa
7. Igreja do Convento do Carmo
8. Casa do Ferreiro das Tabuletas
9. Igreja de São Roque
10. Cerrejaria da Trindade
11. Avenida da Liberdade
12. Mosteiro dos Jerónimos & Torre de Belém
13. Pavilhão do Portugal
14. Estação do Oriente
15. Ponte de Vasco da Gama

This tour introduces you to Lisbon's distinctive buildings representing some of the most prominent architectural styles in the city from the Reconquest to the present, along with a few of my favorite examples. It's not always practical to see them in chronological order, but by the end of the tour you should have a snapshot of the city's turbulent history and occupants through the architectural additions they made. START: **Miradouro de Santa Luzia. Tram: 12, 28. Bus: 37.**

1 ★ Pre-Reconquest Architecture.

The Romans fortified Lisbon from the 3rd century BC, but the only evidence of their occupation remains at the Museu do Teatro Romano, near the Sé (cathedral). With the help of a multi-media show, this highly informative little museum shows you what the Roman theatre looked like (p 58). There's virtually no Moorish architecture (denoting buildings erected by Moors, or

The cathedral, the oldest church in the city.

Muslims of north African origin) either, even though the Moors built on the slopes of the al-Hamma (Alfama) for five centuries (7th–12th). The remains of Moorish houses have been discovered in the grounds of the castle (p 56) and there's a section of Moorish wall leading down the steps from the Miradouro de Santa Luzia to Rua Norberto de Araújo. *Tram 12, 28; Bus 37.*

2 ★ Sé.

The cathedral stands as a monument to Dom Afonso Henrique's Reconquest of Lisbon and is also the city's oldest church. Coming uphill from the Baixa, you will be struck by its two castellated towers, framing the rosette window above the main portal. Once your eyes have adjusted to the darkness inside, you can appreciate the simple Romanesque lines, tall columns topped with a barrel-vaulted ceiling. There are Gothic side chapels, tombs and iron portals too, plus the double arches of the cloisters (it's worth paying to see them). Later embellishments were removed in the 20th century to enhance the cathedral's medieval aspect. 🕐 15–30 min. *Largo da Sé.* ☎ 21-886-6752. Admission free, cloisters 2.50€. Open church daily 9am–7pm; cloisters Oct–Apr only Mon–Sat 10am–6pm, Sun 2pm–6pm. Tram: 12, 28. Bus: 37.

3 ★★ Igreja de Santa Engrácia e Panteão Nacional.

The

The dome of the Panteão Nacional.

The bizarre façade of Casa dos Bicos

building of this church was something of a labor of love, taking almost 300 years to complete (from 1681–1966). Numerous architects built on João Atunes' original design to create the most complete baroque church in Portugal, with curved contours, apses, and dramatic capitals topped with bas relief (carving of a flat surface). Based round a Greek cross, the interior is lined with intricate designs of pink and brown marble, while light filters down from the semi-circular cupola above, the height and light creating a peaceful, cool, and inspiring interior. ⏱ *20–45 min. Campo de Santa Clara.* ☎ *21-1885-4820. www.ippar.pt. Admission 2€, 1€ 15–25 years, 0.80€ student card, free under 15s, plus all on Sun and public holidays. Open Tues–Sun 10am–5pm. Tram: 28. Bus: 9, 25, 35, 39, 46, 81, 90, 104, 105, 107.*

❹ ★ **Casa dos Bicos.** Look out for this bizarre building at the foot of the Alfama, sandwiched between run-down apartments, where lines of washing flutter between the windows. Known in English as the House

Manueline Architecture

Manueline is the most elaborate form of Portuguese architecture. Spanning an approximate 50-year period from 1490 to 1540, it takes its name from Dom Manuel I, who funded construction of churches and monuments with income from the spice trade. Manueline architecture is particularly noted for its ornate, plateresque-style carvings (ornate style with its origins in Spain) with religious, regal, natural and maritime themes, as a celebration of power. Portals, windows, columns and exterior walls display intricate stone carvings of ropes, anchors, armillary spheres (navigational instrument), coats of arms, the cross of the Order of Christ, and natural symbols such as leaves and plants. There was a resurgence of the style during the 19th century, the leading example being Rossio Station (p 67).

Rossio Station is a leading example of 19th-century Neo-Manueline Architecture

of the Points or Spikes, it was built in 1523 by Dom Brás de Albuquerque (1500–80) following a trip to Italy; the texture of the walls have a striking resemblance to the diamond-shaped stones on the Palazzo dei Diamanti in the Italian city of Ferrara. The Casa dos Bicos is rarely open (except for the occasional exhibition), but the façade is the main feature. *Rua dos Bacalhoeiros. Tram: 18, 25. Bus: 9, 28, 35, 81, 82, 90, 746, 759, 794.*

⑤ ★★ Baixa. The neoclassical Baixa district is often referred to as the Baixa Pombalina, a reference to the Marquês de Pombal who spearheaded its construction in the 18th century (p 38). Stretching from the grand expanse of the Praça do Comércio to the Praça de Pedro IV (a.k.a. Rossio) and Praça da Figueira, the easily walked grid-like structure of the Baixa represents a radical departure from the opulent palaces that stood here prior to the 1755 earthquake. As its name suggests, the new Praça do Comércio (Commerce Square) was designated for finance ministries and port authorities, with a symmetrical layout of functional buildings facing inwards, all with arched galleries on the ground floor. One side of the square was left open to the river,

welcoming its trade and the Arco do Triunfo on the opposite side (topped with figures representing glory, valor, and genius) leading to Rua Augusta.

The buildings and streets here are simple and uniform, built for merchants and tradesmen, and the streets retain their original names, such as silver, gold, and shoemaker streets. *Baixa Pombalina. Metro: Baixa-Chiado, Rossio. Tram: 12, 15, 28. Bus: 2, 81, 92.*

Elevador de Santa Justa, which gives access to the Convento do Carmo.

6 ★★ **Elevador de Santa Justa.** This curious, iron structure caught my eye the first time I visited the Baixa. It's hard to miss, as it stands 45 meters high with steps either side leading to the Chiado. It's often called the Elevador do Carmo, as the upper level is used as access to the Convento do Carmo (see right). It has mistakenly been attributed to Gustave Eiffel of Eiffel Tower fame but was actually designed by Porto-born architect Raul Mesnier de Ponsard. Completed in 1902, the structure is neo-gothic with inter-level arched "windows" topped with filigree decoration. It still functions as an elevator (and was recently overhauled), as well as a fun "ride" for visitors. There's a café at the top but it's often crowded. ⏱ *10–20 min. Rua de Santa Justa. Admission 1.30€, free with Carris travel pass. Open winter daily 7am–9pm, summer Mon–Sat 7am–11pm, Sun & public holidays 9am–11pm. Metro: Baixa-Chiado, Rossio. Tram: 15, 28. Bus: 2, 9, 36, 37, 44, 81, 92.*

7 ★★★ **Igreja do Convento do Carmo.** Only the ruins of the church remain of this once-grand 14th-century Carmelite convent, destroyed by the 1755 earthquake and the fire that followed it, but it still exudes a sense of beauty and peace. Despite having no roof, its externals walls remain. Here the tall, narrow arched windows, the Latin-cross layout and bare bones of its arched structure above, reveal its gothic architecture. It's a matter of filling the gaps, with help of the information boards. There's also a small but diverse collection of archeological artifacts, including tombstones with Manueline decoration and Hebrew inscription, a decorated, stone baptismal font, and a baroque tiled panel. ⏱ *30–60 min. Largo do Carmo, 4.* ☎ *21-346-0473. Admission 2.50€, 1.50€ students, seniors, free under 14s & public holidays until 2pm.*

8 **Casa do Ferreiro das Tabuletas.** As you're walking around, you'll notice both functional tiles and elaborate panels decorating

Torre de Belem, a World Heritage Site.

The ruins of Convento de Carmo

both the inside and outside of buildings, a practice developed since the Moorish occupation. You can learn fully about this at the Museu Nacional do Azulejo (National Tile Museum) (see p 51). On this house, you can see an eye-catching example dating from 1864, a building covered in tiles by Luís Ferreira (1807–1870), better known as Ferreira das Tabuletas (Ferreira of the tablets or signs). On each floor there are Romantic figures representing the elements, such as earth and water. *Largo Rafael Bordalo Pinheiro. Elevador da Glória (closed for repairs at time of writing).*

9 Igreja de São Roque. Stop here to see one of the oldest attributed *azulejo* panels in Portugal. Located inside the 15th-century Saint Roque Church, *The Miracle of São Roque* dates approximately to 1584 and is attributed to Francico de Matos and displays Renaissance and Mannerist influences from Italy and Flanders. ⏱ *15–20 min. Largo da Trindade Coelho. Open Mon–Fri 8.30am–5pm, Sat & Sun 9.30am–5pm. Elevador da Glória (closed for repairs at time of writing).*

10 Cervejaria da Trindade. One of my favorite restaurants in Lisbon for the combination of food and relaxed atmosphere, with walls decorated in tiles from the 19th century. At the front of the restaurant the panels reflect the romanticism of the period with images of the seasons, and at the back is a newer panel depicting the monks who once used this as their refectory. *Rua Nova da Trindade.*

Great War statue on Avenida da Liberdade

Vasco da Gama tower in the Parque das Nacoes

☎ 21-342-3506. *Entrees 8€–15€. AE, DC, MC, V. Lunch & dinner daily. Closed public holidays. Elevador da Gloria (closed for repairs at time of writing). Metro: Restauradores.*

⑪ ★★ Avenida da Liberdade.

Built in the 19th century, this avenue stretches from Praça dos Restauradores to Pombal and is a symbol of modernity, a boulevard modeled on the Champs Elysees in Paris. It has a fast, central two-way road, divided from a slow lane by a pedestrianized, tree-lined walkway on either side. It's a pleasure to walk along here, either on the sidewalk looking into the stores, or under the shade of the trees where you can stop for a quiet coffee (p 61). Two of the most iconic buildings are actually in Praça dos Restauradores: the Art Deco Eden Teatro (now an apart-hotel) and the imposing Palácio da Foz (now home to the tourist office).

Metro: Restauradores, Avenida, Pombal. Bus: 2, 9, 36, 44, 45, 90, 91, 711, 732, 746.

⑫ ★★★ Mosteiro dos Jeronimos and kids Torre de Belém.

Two of the most important examples of Manueline architecture (see above), the Jeronimos Monastery and Belém Tower are UNESCO World Heritage Sites and also top of many a tourist schedule (including mine). The Tower is a compact gem of a monument with carved symbols both inside and out, while the Jeronimos Monastery is a monumental treat from its exterior portals, interior columns and vaulted ceilings to its intricate cloisters and choir (p 11). ⏲ *90–120 min. Mosteiro dos Jerónimos, Praça do Império.* ☎ *21-362-0034. www.mosteirodosjeronimos.pt. Admission church free; cloisters and adjoining rooms 4.50€, 2.25€ 15–25 years, 1.80€ youth card holders, free under 15s and general public on Sun & public holidays. Open May–Sep 10am–6.30pm; Oct–Apr 10am–5pm; closed Jan 1, Easter.*

Torre de Belém. Avenida de Brasília. ☎ *21-362-0034. www. mosteirojeronimos.pt/index_torre. html. Admission 3€, 1.50€ kids 4–15 years & seniors, 1.20€ youth card holders, free under 14s, general public Sun & public holidays until 2pm. Open Oct–Apr Tues–Sun 10am–5pm; May–Sep Tues–Sun 10am–6.30pm. Train: Belém. Tram: 15. Bus: 27, 28, 29, 43, 49, 51, 112.*

⑬ ★ Pavilhão de Portugal.

Designed for the 1998 Expo by one of my favorite contemporary architects, Álvaro Siza Vieira, the Portugal Pavilion is a showcase of modern Lisbon. My excitement isn't focused on the main building but on the open space in front. It is covered by a large concrete roof that appears like a draped sheet, a feat that has astounded many an

Estação do Oriente.

engineer. I also like the front of the building for its sharp lines and angles, along with the matching supporting wall at the far end. It turns the idea of a façade on its head, as the main entrance is located at the side of the building, keeping the focus on the public spaces, rather than projecting importance on those inside. *Cais Português, Doca dos Olivais. Metro & Train: Oriente. Bus: 5, 25, 750, 759, 794.*

⓮ ★ **Estação do Oriente.** It might sound eccentric, but I love visiting Parque das Nações' train station. No, I'm not a trainspotter, this is an architectural attraction in itself. Designed by Spaniard Santiago Calatrava, the most striking feature is the platform level, a combination of metal and glass columns and roof which resemble a forest of palms. *Metro & Train: Oriente. Bus: 5, 25, 750, 759, 794.*

⓯ ★★ **Ponte de Vasco de Gama.** A fast alternative route for those heading to and from the south, this bridge keeps traffic out of the city center. What's more, Lisbon's 25 de Abril Bridge was built during the

Salazar dictatorship and was named after him until the Carnation Revolution (p 37), when it took the day's date. So while that is a reminder of the past, the Vasco da Gama Bridge represents the future—a sleek, concrete construction that snakes 12km across the tidal waters of the Tagus River. Although at the far end of the Parque das Nações, you should try and see it close up—I recommend a trip to the viewing platform of the Vasco da Gama Tower for a bird's-eye view. *Metro & Train: Oriente. Bus: 5, 25, 750, 759, 794.*

The Art Deco Eden Teatro on Avenida da Liberdade.

Child's Play: Lisbon with Kids

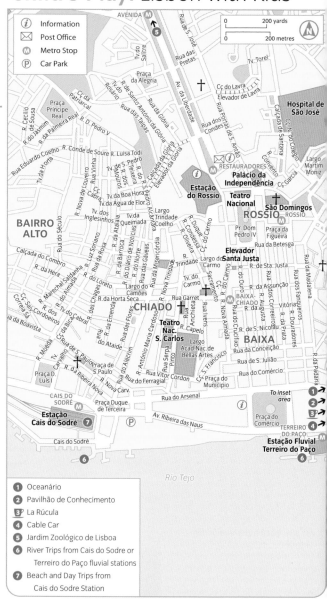

- ⓘ Information
- ⊠ Post Office
- Ⓜ Metro Stop
- Ⓟ Car Park

1. Oceanário
2. Pavilhão de Conhecimento
3. La Rúcula
4. Cable Car
5. Jardim Zoológico de Lisboa
6. River Trips from Cais do Sodre or Terreiro do Paço fluvial stations
7. Beach and Day Trips from Cais do Sodre Station

Taking kids to the city doesn't have to be a pain, not if you know where to go and what will keep them happy. This tour guides you round some of the best child-friendly museums, attractions, and activities from Parque das Nações to the Jardim Zoológico de Lisboa or a boat trip and a day at the beach. START: **Parque das Nações. Metro: Oriente. Bus: 5, 10, 19, 21, 28, 50 ,68, 81, 82, 85.**

1 ★★★ Oceanário. An expensive but worthwhile attraction: I'd definitely dive deep into my purse for the tickets to the Oceanarium. There's an easy-to-follow route, so you won't easily lose the kids. Most of them will love it, as they can get close to big sharks, see cute otters, and learn about strange underwater creatures such as the sea dragon, which looks like a piece of drifting seaweed. At the end there's a shop where they can buy a cuddly octopus, marine-theme pencils and all kinds of books, games and toys. ⏱ *60–90 min. Doca dos Olivais.;* ☎ *21-891-7002. www.oceanario.pt. Admission 10.50€, 5.75€ seniors, 5.12€ kids 4–12, free under 3s. Open Apr–Oct daily 10am–7pm, Nov–Mar daily 10am–6pm, Dec 25 1pm–6pm, New Year's Day 12–6pm. Metro & Train: Oriente. Bus: 5, 10, 19, 21, 28, 50 ,68, 81, 82, 85.*

2 ★★ Pavilhão de Conhecimento. Just a short walk from the Oceanario, the Knowledge Pavilion brims with the kind of interactive science and knowledge exhibits that kids love to fiddle with. The permanent exhibits are divided into four sections with something for children of all ages and abilities, and I find it hard to choose my favorite. I wasn't allowed in **The Unfinished House**—as this is for kids of 3–6 years only, but from the racket inside you know they're having a ball; they are supervised as they play and help build a house with foam bricks. **Exploratorium** introduces kids to natural elements from tornadoes to soap bubbles. **See, Do, Learn,** on the other hand explores our own physical abilities, such as the energy needed to blow up a hot air balloon. **Live Mathematics** is better than it sounds,

Kids will love the otters at Oceanario.

Parque das Nações—getting around

At Nations' Park, there are various options to ease those tired young feet. As well as the cable car (see below), there's a tourist mini-train that starts and finishes at Alameda dos Oceanos (by the Pavilhão Atlântico). Admission 2.50€, 1.50€ kids 5–12, seniors, free under 5s. Open Jul–Sep 10am–7pm, Oct–Jun 10am–5pm.

Kids might not want to walk but are often keen to pedal, so try hiring bicycles and go-karts from Tejo Bike. They have two outlets here, one by the Pavilhão Atlântico, the other by Sony Park towards the bridge. Bikes can be hired from ½ to 10 hours and there are many safe routes around the site. www.tejobike.pt. Price bicycles 2.25€ adults, 1.50€ kids, go-karts 3€, 2.50€ kids, 6.80€ family go-kart. Open Mar–Oct 10am–8pm, Nov–Feb 11am–6pm.

with fun ways of playing with numbers. There are regular temporary exhibitions here too. ⏱ *60–90 min. Alameda dos Oceanos.* ☎ *21-891-7100. www. pavconhecimento.pt. Admission 6€, 3€ seniors; kids 7–17, 2.50€ kids 3–6, free under 3s, 13€ families (1 or 2 adults with kids up to 17 years). Open Tues–Fri 10am–6pm, weekends & public holidays 11am–7pm. Metro & Train: Oriente. Bus: 5, 10, 19, 21, 28, 50 ,68, 81, 82, 85.*

3 ★★ **La Rúcula.** Eating Italian is a quick and easy option to keep the whole family happy without breaking the bank. This modern restaurant opposite the Atlantic Pavilion has oven-baked pizzas, pasta, salads, steaks, and a long list of delicious Italian desserts from tiramisu to chocolate tart. *Rossio dos Olivais* ☎ *21-892-2747. $$.*

The cable car at Parque das Nações.

Tagus River boat trip

④ ★ Cable car. Unless your kids are petrified of heights, they'll find the cable car is a thrill, and a quick way to get from one end of the park to the other. Kids get to literally hop on the car as passes through the station (don't worry, it's very slow), the doors close and the car rises over the buildings. Take a map and point out the different attractions, from the Oceanário and bulbous Pavilhão Atlântico to the Vasco da Gama Bridge. If you have a return, you can either hop off and return later, or stay on for a circular trip. ⏱ *10–20 min. Between Doca dos Olivais and Torre de Vasco da Gama. ☎ 21-895-6143. www.parquedas nacoes.pt. Admission 3.50€ one way, 5.50€ round trip, 1.80€ kids 5–14, seniors one way, 3€ kids 5–14, seniors round trip, free under 5s. Open Oct–May Mon–Fri 11am–7pm, Sat, Sun & public holidays 10am–8pm; Jun–Sep Mon–Fri 11am–8pm, Sat, Sun & public holidays 10am–9pm. Metro & Train: Oriente. Bus: 5, 25, 28, 44, 708, 750, 759, 794.*

⑤ ★★ Jardim Zoológico de Lisboa. Most kids love zoos and as Lisbon's is open every day of the

Parque das Nações Playgrounds

Nations' Park has several specially designed play areas for kids of various ages. The Music Playground (at Passeio das Tágides, next to Garcia Horta Gardens) is an intriguing space with several bronze "instruments" ranging from triangles and gongs to musical columns. Kids are free to jump on them to discover the different sounds that they make.

The Parque do Tejo Playground in the Tagus Gardens Park is more of a classic space and designed to keep kids of different ages occupied. On one side there's a sandy area with wooden animals, slides, and a small climbing wall. On the other side, Pirâmide do Gil has a pyramid made from metal and rope, which seems to attract kids like a magnet as they are pulled by the challenge of getting to the top.

Hippos at Lisbon's Zoo.

year, it's always an option. There's everything from cheeky chimpanzees and huge hippopotami to tropical birds, reptiles, and plenty of creepy crawlies. The best parts though are the feeding and demos, so try and coordinate your visit with these. You can, of course, spend all day here with entertainment and eating at Animax. Try and distract the kids, though, as it's right by the entrance to the zoo and you might

Vasco de Gama Shopping Center

not want them haggling for an ice cream right away. 🕐 *60–180 min. Sete Rios, Praça Marechal Humberto Delgado.* ☎ *21-723-2920. www.zoo. pt. Admission 14.50€, 12€ seniors, 11€ kids 3–11, free under 3s. Open daily 10am–8pm; dolphin and sea lion presentation Wed–Mon 11am & 3pm, Tue 3pm; sea-lion feeding daily 10.30am & 2pm; pelican feeding daily 2.30pm; free-flying bird demo daily 12.30pm & 4.30pm.*

⑥ ★★ Tagus River boat trip.
During the hot summer, what could be better than an ice cream for cooling your kids off as you glide along? Boat trips are a novelty and give kids a new view from the water. It doesn't have to be expensive, as you can opt for the Transtejo river buses that run from Cais do Sodre, Terreiro do Paço, and Belém to locations on the other side. One of the best routes is to Cacilhas, from where you can take them on a bus trip to the Cristo do Rei statue (p 43). If you want more than a quick taster, take one of the tourist boats, which depart from Terreiro do Paço daily at 3pm. The trips take 2½ hours and take in various sights

Eating and Entertainment

There's no shortage of eateries throughout Lisbon (p 105) but shopping centers are my top choice, especially on a rainy day. The food section at such locations is a revelation—although you'll get the usual fast-food chains, there are also healthy options, sandwiches, smoothies, ice cream and full hot meals, mostly at a good price. The city's three main shopping centers, Vasco da Gama, Colombo and Amoreiras, also all have multi-screen movie theaters, and movies here are often in English with Portuguese subtitles (do ask first).

along the river, but you will pay quite a lot more. ⏱ *20–120 min. Fluvial stations: Cais do Sodré, Terreiro do Paço, Belém.* ☎ *808-203-050. www.transtejo.pt. Riverbus 0.74€–1.95€, 0.80€–0.98€ kids. Tourist boat 20€, 10€ kids, seniors. First and last (different routes vary) 5.15am–2.30am.*

7 ★★ **Beach and Day Trips.**
It's not exactly unknown for kids to ask to go to the beach. Fortunately from Lisbon, it's an easy trip. Trains leave regularly from Cais do Sodré to the Estoril coast, where you have a choice of good beaches to choose from (p 150). Trains from Oriente and Entrecampos run to Sintra, which kids will love with its fantasy palaces, Moorish castle, and toy museum (p 158).

Historic Sintra, an easy day trip from Lisbon.

Lisbon's **Heroes**

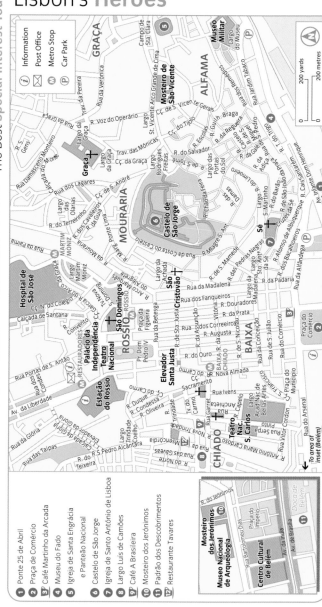

Legend

- ⓘ Information
- ✉ Post Office
- Ⓜ Metro Stop
- Ⓟ Car Park

200 yards
200 metres

Map labels:

GRAÇA
ALFAMA
MOURARIA
BAIXA
CHIADO
ROSSIO

Museu Militar
Campo de Sta. Clara
Mosteiro de São Vicente
Castelo de São Jorge
São Cristovão
Sé
Hospital de São José
São Domingos
Palácio da Independência
Teatro Nacional
Estação do Rossio
Elevador Santa Justa
Teatro Nac. S. Carlos
Praça do Comércio

Mosteiro dos Jerónimos
Museu Nacional de Arqueologia
Centro Cultural de Belém

To area of Inset (Belém)

List of numbered sites:

1. Ponte 25 de Abril
2. Praça de Comércio
3. Café Martinho da Arcada
4. Museu do Fado
5. Igreja de Santa Engrácia e Panteão Nacional
6. Castelo de São Jorge
7. Igreja de Santo António de Lisboa
8. Largo Luís de Camões
9. Café A Brasileira
10. Mosteiro dos Jerónimos
11. Padrão dos Descobrimentos
12. Restaurante Tavares

Lisbon has paid tribute to some of its heroes who have played an important part in its unique identity. This tour gives you plenty of insight into the city's personalities, from kings and the patron saint to poets and singers. It gives a refreshing new slant on some of Lisbon's major attractions as well as some lesser known corners. START: **Praça do Comércio. Metro: Baixa/Chiado. Tram: 12, 15. Bus: 2, 81, 92, 711, 713.**

❶ ★ **Ponte 25 de Abril.** This striking red suspension bridge runs from Lisbon to Almada, where the Cristo Rei statue stands, arms wide. When it was inaugurated in 1966, it was named after the dictator, Salazar, who led the right-wing *Estado Novo* (new state) here for 36 years. It was renamed after the date of the Carnation Revolution, when the dictatorship was brought to a peaceful end in a bloodless, left-wing coup, led by the military. On April 25, 1974 they came out onto the streets, joined by thousands of the general public who brought carnations from the market. To me, the bridge pays homage to all the heroes of the revolution, the Portuguese people who brought democracy to the country.

🕑 *20 mins. Train Alcântara; Tram 15; Bus 27, 28, 29, 43, 49, 51, 112.*

Dom Jose, king at the time of the 1755 earthquake.

❷ ★★ **Praça de Comércio.** I've placed Praça de Comércio near the start of this tour to make a point. The center of the square is dominated by a bronze of Dom Jose I (king from 1750–77), commissioned by Pombal (see below) as a homage to the king for rebuilding the city after the earthquake of 1755. It was Pombal who took control of the reconstruction, creating this airy neo-classical square surrounded by arches and the grid-like Baixa north of it. As well as the statue itself, look at the pedestal—determined to be remembered, he inserted a bronze medallion of himself as the real force behind the new direction for the city. *Metro: Baixa-Chiado. Tram: 12, 15, 25. Bus: 2, 81, 92.*

The 200-year-old Café Martinho da Arcada.

❸ **Café Martinho da Arcada.** This 200-year-old café and restaurant exudes 19th-century Portuguese elegance—rich dark wood, tiles and mirrors, and the aroma of fresh coffee and cakes beckoning from the counter. Fernando Pessoa (see below) was a regular and there is a corner dedicated to him in the restaurant, his picture on the wall, and a coffee cup and books on the table beside it. *Praça do Comércio, 3.* ☎ *21-887-9259. Open 8am–11pm Mon–Sat. Tram: 12, 15. $$$*

④ ★★ Museu do Fado.

Both a museum and cultural center, this is the key place for learning more about all aspects of *fado*, Portugal's haunting and very distinctive genre of melancholy folk song. Located at the foot of the Alfama, the permanent exhibition explores the development from the 19th century to the present with collections of Portuguese guitars, and a prized collection of brochures, posters and photos. Look out for pieces on such stars as Maria Severa, Maria do Carmo and guitarist Carlos Paredes

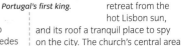

Dom Alfonso Henriques, Portugal's first king.

as well as Amália Rodrigues (see below), as well as contemporary singers such as Mariza. ⏰ *30–45 min. Largo do Chafariz.* ☎ *21-882-3470. Admission 3€, 1.50€ kids 4–18 years & students with ID, 1.75€ Lisboa Card. Open 10am–6pm Tues–Sat. Bus: 9, 28, 35, 81, 82.*

⑤ ★★ Igreja de Santa Engrácia e Panteao Nacional.

The tombs and cenotaphs inside the National Pantheon read like a who's who of Lisbon's (and Portugal's) history. It's not macabre though; this is a masterpiece of Portuguese baroque architecture, its marble interiors a cool retreat from the hot Lisbon sun, and its roof a tranquil place to spy on the city. The church's central area

Three Heroes

Born in Lisbon as Sebastião José Cavalho e Melo, Marquês de **Pombal** (1699–1782) was prime minister from 1750–77. He is most remembered in Lisbon for spearheading the rebuilding of the city after the earthquake, replacing the luxurious waterfront palaces with the neo-classical Baixa, built for the merchant classes and tradesmen.

Fernando Pessoa (1888–1935) became part of the vanguard of modern literature, meeting with other writers in Café Martinho da Arcada and A Brasileira, and is most renowned for writing under heteronyms. The most famous of these are Ricardo Reis and Bernardo Soares, and his best works are considered to be The Book of Disquiet and Message.

Amália Rodrigues (1920–99) helped shape modern fado music and many of her recordings are used as standards for the genre. She first sang professionally in 1939 and appeared in movies such as Capas Negras (1947). She released her final album, Segredo, two years before she died.

St Anthony, patron saint of Lisbon.

(in the shape of a Greek cross) includes cenotaphs dedicated to writer Luís de Camões (c.1524–80) and explorer Vasco da Gama (c.1460–1524), and four corner rooms house the tombs of former presidents, writers, and other personalities. The most touching one is that of *fado* singer Amália Rodrigues; she's the only woman entombed at the pantheon and there are often fresh flowers around it. ⏱ *20–45 min. Campo de Santa Clara.* ☎ *21-885-4820. Admission 2€, 1€ 15–25 years, 0.80€ student card, free under 15s, plus all on Sunday and public holidays. Open Tues–Sun 10am–5pm. Tram: 28. Bus: 12, 34.*

⑥ ★★★ Castelo de São Jorge.
Of course Lisbon's castle is a must-see on any trip to the city (see p 8 and p 56) but when you're there, seek out the statue of Dom Afonso Henriques (1109–85) in the Praça das Armas, the large, cool and leafy square just through the turnstiles that offers breathtaking views across the city. Portugal's first king, he drove the Moors out of the city in 1147. Dressed in mail armor, his sword raised and his shield bearing a cross, he appears powerful and strong, a crusading king who led his men from the front and now stands surveying his prize. ⏱ *60–90 min. Alfama.* ☎ *21-880-0620. www.castelosaojorge.egeac.pt. Admission 5€, 30% discount Lisboa Card, free under 10s & seniors. Open Nov–Feb 9am–6pm; Mar–Oct 9am–9pm. Tram: 12, 28. Bus: 37.*

⑦ ★ Igreja de Santo António de Lisboa. This church is dedicated to St. Anthony (1195–1231), the patron saint of Lisbon. Located in a tree-lined square close to the Sé (cathedral), on the site of the house where the saint's parents lived, the church is a favorite for local weddings. Not much remains of the original church but the reconstruction is simple and attractive with white, pink and yellow marble inlays—go inside for a few moments of contemplation or relax in the square where there's a typical statue of St. Anthony holding a child. This area comes alive during the week before and after the St. Anthony's Day celebrations on June 13, when the area buzzes with. impromptu bars, *fado* music, grilled sardines, and plenty of wine. ⏱ *10–15 min. Largo de Santo António da Sé.* ☎ *21-886-9145. Admission free. Open daily 8am–7.30pm. Tram: 12, 28. Bus: 37.*

⑧ ★ Largo Luis de Camões.
At the juncture between the Chiado and the Bairro Alto proper, this is really a passing-through point, with tram-stops, shops and cafés on either side. At its center is a statue of Luis de Camões (see below), Portugal's most renowned writer, after whom the square is named. *Metro: Baixa-Chiado. Bairro Alto. Tram: 28. Bus: 58, 92, 790.*

Vasco da Gama & Luís Vaz de Camões

Vasco da Gama (c. 1460–1524) is one of the most notable figures in Portugal's Golden Age of Discovery. He established a sea route to India, making all the seafaring "discoveries" of his predecessors worthwhile, as there was now no need for goods to be brought via the arduous Silk Road through the Middle East.

Luís Vaz de Camões (c.1524–80), born in Lisbon, is also connected with the discoveries, but through writing. Living a life on the edge, he took part in military expeditions, lost his right eye in Ceuta, bedded many a court lady, and was sent to Goa after injuring a member of the Royal Stables. He wrote his most famous work, Os Lusiadas (The Lusiads), while in Macau, an epic poem that charts Portuguese history, focusing on Vasco da Gama's trip to India.

9 ★★ **A Brasileira.** This café is among the best known in Lisbon and located on a well-trodden tourist route. Crowds of people hang round to see the striking bronze statue of Fernando Pessoa seated outside the café. It's a pleasant place to sit in the summer months and contemplate the lives of struggling writers in 1920s' Lisbon. But do venture inside and chat to the waiters—they'll indicate the table where groups of artists and writers still meet at 10am each morning. *Rua Garrett 100-122.* ☎ *21-346-9541. Open daily 8am–2am. Metro: Baixa-Chiado, Bairro Alto. Tram: 28. Bus: 58, 92, 790.*

10 ★★★ **Mosteiro dos Jeronimos.** Take tram 15 to Belém to see one of the most celebrated monuments in the city. As an example of Manueline architecture (see p 24) this (along with the Torre de Belém by the river—see p 72) is one of the most

prized examples. As you enter the main portal, you'll see two elaborate tombs. On the left is Fernando Pessoa and on the right the explorer Vasco da Gama. In the summer it can get overrun with noisy tours and flashing cameras, so if you want to find peace in the church and the space to examine the elaborate décor, come in low season. ⏱ *60–90 min. Praça do Império.* ☎ *21-362-0034. www.mosteirodos jeronimos.pt. Admission church free; cloisters and adjoining rooms 4.50€, 2.25€ 15–25 years, 1.80€ youth card holders, free under 15s and general public on Sun & public holidays. Open May–Sep 10am–6.30pm; Oct–Apr 10am–5pm; closed Jan 1, Easter Sunday, May 1, Dec 25. Tram: 15. Bus: 714, 727, 729, 751.*

Luis de Camoes tomb inside Jeronimos Monastery

Padrão dos Descobrimentos with Henry the Navigator at the bow.

⑪ ★★★ Padrão dos Descobrimentos. The Discoveries Monument is one of the most iconic monuments in Lisbon, appearing on many a guidebook cover. Towering more than 50 meters high and located on the edge of the Tagus River, it was built in 1960 for the 500th anniversary of the death of Henry the Navigator and as a homage to those that took part in the Golden Age of Discovery. It takes the form of a *caravela*, the ships used by Portuguese seafarers, its sails billowing above in the wind. On its bow stand Henry the Navigator, Vasco da Gama, Pedro Alvares Cabral, Ferdinand Magellan, Diogo Cão, Afonso de Albuquerque, Luis de Camões, and Dom Manuel I, among others. There's seating around the sculpture, a good place to rest before heading back into the city center. ⏱ *10–30 min.*

Avenida de Brasília. ☎ *21-303-1950. www.padraodescobrimentos. egeac.pt. Admission 2.50€; 1.50€ kids 12–18, students under 25, 6€ families (2+2). Open May–Sep 10am–7pm Tues–Sun; Oct–Apr 10am–6pm Tues–Sun. Tram: 15. Bus: 714, 727, 729, 751.*

⑫ Restaurante Tavares BAIRRO ALTO   Tavares is Lisbon's oldest restaurant and famed for having once been a hang-out of renowned writers such as such as Eça de Queiros. It's not a cheap restaurant by Portuguese standards but worth it to be met by a uniformed doorman, take in the palatial interiors and sample the international gastronomy. *R da Miseracordia.* ☎ *21-342-1112. Entrees 45€–60€; tasting menu 65€. AE, DC, MC, V. Dinner. Tram 28. Map p 102.*

True Romance

1 Tagus Boat Trips
2 Monumento a Cristo Rei
3 Castelo de São Jorge
4 Restaurante Casa do Leão
5 Miradouro de Santa Luzia
6 Jardim Botânico
7 Solar do Vinho do Porto

(i) Information
✉ Post Office
Ⓜ Metro Stop
Ⓟ Car Park

Lisbon has plenty of places where you have time to walk, talk, cozy up in a quiet restaurant and look across the city in all its astonishing variety. On this tour you will encounter classic vantage points that will stay in the memory, offering plenty of scope for sharing moments to savor the seductive qualities of the city, from the shade of the Jardim Botânico to a quiet drink in the Solar.

START: **Terreiro do Paço fluvial station. Tram: 15, 18, 25. Bus: 2, 81, 92, 711, 713. Cais do Sodré fluvial station. Tram: 15, 18, 25. Bus: 6, 35, 36, 40, 44, 45, 58, 82, 91.**

① ★★ kids **Tagus boat trip.**
Whether it's summer or winter, you can snuggle up together on one of Transtejo's tourist boats along the Tagus river, which leave from the Fluvial station at Terreiro do Paço daily at 3pm. There are plenty of views in the city but there's something about seeing a place from the river that I really enjoy— the boat might be packed, but you feel separated from the hustle of city life and see the sights from a different perspective. If you're going to the Cristo Rei (see below) you can hop on a river bus, which is relatively quick and much cheaper. ⏱ *10–120 min. Fluvial stations: Terreiro do Paço or Cais do Sodré for Cacilhas, Terreiro do Paço for the tourist boat.* ☎ *808-203 -050. www.transtejo.pt.*

Riverbus 0.74€–1.95€; 0.80€–0.98€; tourist boat 20€; 10€ kids, seniors. First and last river bus 5.15am– 2.30am; tourist boat daily 3pm.

② ★★ kids **Monumento a Cristo Rei.** One of the city's great landmarks, the Statue of Christ the King is actually in Almada on the south side of the Tagus. Either take an organized bus tour or hop on a riverbus from Cais do Sodré to Cacilhas (see above) and then take bus no.101 (approximately every 20 min.) from outside the fluvial station to the Cristo Rei front gates. Buy a ticket and take the elevator to the top of the statue. Around 110 meters high, it is based on a similar one that looks down from Corcovado mountain over Rio de Janeiro,

Monumenta a Cristo Rei.

Brazil. Once out of the elevator, climb a few more steps to the very top— it can get windy up there, so hold onto each other for good measure. It's good to get here at the latest by mid-morning so you can get back to Lisbon for lunch. On a clear summer's day, the sun is behind the statue in late morning so you have superb views (good light for photos) of the 25 de Abril Bridge below and the Lisbon panorama beyond. What's more, when the sun is directly behind the head of the statue, it appears like a glowing halo. ◷ *30–60 min. plus 45 min. return trip by ferry and bus. Alto de Pragal, Almada.* ☎ *21-275-1000. www.cristo-rei.com. Admission 4€, 2€ under 8s. Open daily 9.30am–6pm. Bus:101 from Cacilhas.*

③ ★★★ Castelo de São Jorge.
One of Lisbon's most notable attractions, perched on top of the Alfama hill, St. George's Castle is mostly a modern reconstruction (p 8 and p 39), which some find reason to criticize. But immerse yourself in thoughts of where you are, think about the fact that it lies at the ancient heart of Lisbon, from where Romans, Moors and Portuguese kings guarded their city for centuries,

and you'll discover the romance of this place—much of it unchanged through centuries—and panoramas across the city. Head up here after lunch, when most of the tourist coaches have dashed off elsewhere. Or come here for lunch (see below) and then wander through the shade of the Praça das Armas, climb the turrets for ever-better views, and wander back through the cobbled streets of Santa Cruz, the district within the castle walls, with whitewashed houses and small souvenir shops that give it a village feel. ◷ *60–90 min. Alfama.* ☎ *21-880-0620. www. castelosaojorge.egeac.pt. Admission 5€, 30% discount Lisboa Card, free under 10s, seniors. Open Nov–Feb 9am–6pm, Mar–Oct 9am–9pm. Tram: 12, 28. Bus: 37.*

④ Restaurante Casa do Leão.
Located inside St. George's Castle, the Casa do Leão has carefully incorporated the vaulted brick ceiling of the former palace with a tiled bar and elegant figures on the wall. Book a table for a romantic lunch (or dinner) and take your time over its menu of Portuguese and international cuisine, from local bacalhau

Castelo de São Jorge crowns the ancient Alfama district.

Jardin Botânico, a cool haven in the middle of the day.

to juicy steaks. *Castelo de São Jorge.* ☎ *21-888-0154. www.pousadas.pt. Open daily 12.30–3pm & 8–11pm. $$$$.*

⑤ Miradouro de Santa Luzia.

Stroll back down from the castle and stop at this viewing point. I keep coming back here to peek through the port-holes in the white wall, which frame the river like a landscape painting. At either end of the wall are a small church run by the Order of Malta (see p 58) and large tiled panel of the city, while to the left (as you face the river) the Portas do Sol viewing point opens out onto a bright esplanade where you can stop for coffee. Walk back downhill to the Baixa, where you can hop on a metro to Rato. ⏱ *10–20 min. Alfama. Open all day. Tram: 12, 28. Bus: 37.*

⑥ ★★ Jardim Botânico.

Tucked away behind the Museu Nacional de História Nacional, the Botanic Garden is a city oasis. I love the afternoons here, where the heat is taken out of the day, the tall tropical trees rise above your head, and the sun trickles through the leaves. A warren of mosaic pathways and steps, palms and magnolia trees, you can sit on a bench by a pond of water lilies and only just be aware of the distant hum of the traffic. ⏱ *45–120 min. Rua da Escola Politécnica, 58.* ☎ *21-392-1800. www.jb.ul.pt. Admission 1.50€, 0.75€ seniors, students, youth card holders, free under 6s. Open Apr–Oct Mon–Fri 9am–8pm, Sat & Sun 10am–8pm; Nov–Mar Mon–Fri 9am–6pm, Sat & Sun 10am–6pm. Bus: 58 (stops outside entrance), 92, 711, 790. Metro: Rato.*

⑦ Solar do Vinho do Porto.

Always a special place to come to, but I like it above all for the pre-dinner drinks. It occupies a former palace, and its low lights, stone walls and deep sofas give instant relief to those aching feet, and a glass of port warms the insides like soft velvet. It's also a peaceful place for an intimate chat. Select a corner, choose from the menu of ports and accompany it with a few savory nibbles. *Rua de São Pedro de Alcântara, 45.* ☎ *21-347-5707. www.ivp.pt. Open Mon–Sat 11am–12am.*

Art Club

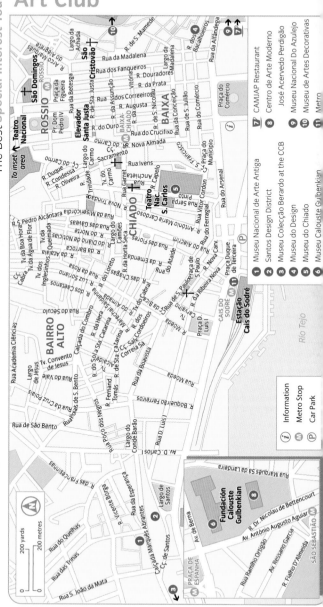

1 Museu Nacional de Arte Antiga
2 Santos Design District
3 Museu Colecção Berardo at the CCB
4 Museu do Design
5 Museu do Chiado
6 Museu Calouste Gulbenkian
7 CAMJAP Restaurant
8 Centro de Arte Moderno
  José Acevedo Perdigão
9 Museu Nacional Do Azulejo
10 Museu de Artes Decorativas
11 Metro

ⓘ Information
Ⓜ Metro Stop
Ⓟ Car Park

Fundación Calouste Gulbenkian

BAIRRO ALTO
CHIADO
BAIXA
ROSSIO

Rio Tejo

Τhis tour takes in the best of Lisbon's art collections, but some of them are so vast you'll probably have to spread it over a couple of days or pick out a few pictures to examine closely. There's everything from ancient religious painting from the Middle Ages and decorative art from the Far East to contemporary Portuguese installations and design, so use this as a guide and choose according to your own favorite artistic periods and styles.

START: **Museu Nacional de Arte Antiga. Tram: 15, 28. Bus: 6, 28, 60, 713, 714, 727, 794.**

① ★★★ **Museu Nacional de Arte Antiga.** You need at least an hour to see the National Museum of Ancient Art's highlights, more if you want to appreciate it fully. It's considered the most important museum in the country for both the value and chronological breadth of its collection. I've found it an eye-opener revealing the wealth and quality of art from Portugal itself. There are vast collections of work dating from 8th–19th centuries, so you'll need to be selective, but I suggest the Portuguese and European paintings, which are at the heart of the collection. The large vibrant paintings of St. Vincent attributed to Portuguese Renaissance artist Nuno Gonçalves (active 1450–71) are particularly outstanding, along with

the 13th- and 14th-century Portuguese sculptures in wood and gilt, and the Dutch Still Lifes. The Art of the Portuguese Expansion includes everything from elaborate hand-painted screens from China to Indian furniture and African masks. *Rua das Janelas Verdes.* ⏱ *60–90 min.* ☎ *21-391-2800. www.mnarteantiga-ipmuseus.pt. Admission 3€, 60% discount youth card holders, 50% discount 15–25 years & seniors, free under 14s & on Sun and public holidays. Open Tues 2pm–6pm, Wed–Sun 10am–6pm. Tram: 15, 28. Bus: 6, 28, 60, 713, 714, 727, 794.*

② ★ **Santos Design District.** Santos is the area between the MNAA and the Mercado da Ribeira

Museu Nacional de Arte Antiga.

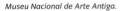

Museu Colecção Berardo de Arte Moderna e Contemporânea.

in Praça Dom Luis spread along the riverfront inland a few blocks. Once an industrial area, today it's the in place to explore and the avant-garde design district. It's fast becoming a favorite haunt for eating and drinking. Santos also has its fair share of museums, including MNAA, Museu das Comunicações and

Chinese porcelain on display at Museu Calouste Gulbenkian

Museu da Marioneta. If you want to stay here, York House is a boutique hotel in a former town house that combines traditional charm with modern comforts (p 148). *Tram: 15, 28. Bus: 6, 28, 60, 714, 732.*

❸ ★★ **Museu Colecção Berardo de Arte Moderna e Contemporânea.** In 2007, the Berardo Collection of Contemporary and Modern Art opened at the Belém Cultural Center (CCB). At first I was sorry that the CCB had ended its era of hosting top-notch, temporary exhibitions and being home to the Design Museum (see above), but on visiting the recently opened Berardo Collection, it was apparent it was offering a comprehensive, international, permanent and developing overview of modern and contemporary art—and it's free (at the time of writing). The museum is displaying its collection of more than 860 pieces (and rising) by rotation, according to artistic movement from the 20th-century to the present. You can expect works by Pablo Picasso, Salvador Dalí, Marcel Duchamp, Francis Bacon, Max Ernst, and plenty of rising stars. Either drop in or check out their program in advance to see what's on display. ⏱ *60–90 min. Praça do Imperio.* ☎ *21-361-2400.*

www.museuberardo.com. Admission free at time of writing, but phone for latest charges. Open daily 10am–6pm (Fri until 10pm). Tours in English, 4pm Sat. Train: Belém. Tram: 15. Bus: 27, 28, 29, 43, 49, 51, 112.

④ ★★ **Museu do Design.** At the time of writing Lisbon's superb Design Museum had closed, and a new Museum of Design and Fashion or MuDe (*mude* means "change" in Portuguese) was scheduled to be installed in 2009 in the Palácio Verride, a former palace at the Santa Catarina viewing point. The plan is to combine more than 1,200 couture pieces with the existing design collection. This includes pieces by design luminaries such as André Arbus and Frank O. Gehry. While it is waiting for its new home, there are temporary displays of the collection at the Sala do Risco.
🕐 45–60 min.*Sala do Risco, Largo de San António da Sé (Alfama.)*
☎ *21-888-6117. www.mude.pt (under construction). Admission free. Open daily 10am–6pm (Fri until 10pm). Tram: 12, 28. Bus: 37.*

⑤ ★ **Museu do Chiado.** If you like the Modernists (well, from the Romantic movement to the present), then this is the place to see

Museu de Chiado.

painting and architecture in Lisbon. First opened in 1911, it gained a new home in 1994 following the Chiado fire eight years earlier. The neo-modern building's airy reception is inviting and you can enjoy the collection at your leisure, surrounded by the unusual bluish light that reflects from the Cascais stone floors. However, the lack of space means the museum presents its collection on constant rotation. So you're as likely to see a retrospective of 19th-century Portuguese art

Museu Calouste Gulbenkian.

as you are works from the 1990s and contemporary period. ⏱ *45–60 min. Rua Serpa Pinto 4.* ☎ *21-343-2148. www.museudochiado-ip museus.pt. Admission 3€, 50% discount 15–25 years & seniors, 60% youth card holders, 20% discount TAP passengers with boarding card, free under 14s & Lisboa Card. Open Tues–Sun 10am–6pm. Tram: 28. Metro: Baixa-Chiado. Bus: 58, 100.*

6 ★★★ **Museu Calouste Gulbenkian.** Owing its existence to collector and benefactor Calouste Sarkis Gulbenkian (p 17), this museum appeals to wide tastes, with a little of everything from Egyptian sculpture and Oriental decorative arts to fine European paintings. It's the kind of museum you can return to again and again, and relax in the lush gardens outside. Amongst its treasures is a superb collection of Islamic Art comprising hand-painted ceramics with geometric designs, glazed tiles, prayer niches and mosque lamps with engraved passages from the Qur'an. The Persian silks and an Armenian bible, with painted illustrations inlaid with gilt,

are also particularly special. Amongst the European art you'll find everything from an elaborate 14th-century carved diptych of the Passion of Christ to the French sculptor August Rodin's *Jean D'Aire, Burgher of Calais*, plus a fine selection of paintings by Rousseau, Manet, Degas, Renoir, and Monet. ⏱ *60–120 min. Avenida de Berna, 45A.* ☎ *21-782-3000. www.museu.gulbenkian.pt. Admission 4€, 20% discount Lisboa Card, 50% discount seniors & students, free under 12s. Open Tues–Sun 10am–5.45pm. Metro: São Sebastião, Praça de Espanha. Bus: 16, 26, 31, 46, 56.*

7 **CAMJAP Restaurant.** Not only is this a convenient stop-off when you're visiting several museums, but you can get a good hot meal here for around 6.50€. There's a self-service buffet, or you can just have a coffee and enjoy the view over the CAMJAP museum garden. *Rua Madre de Deus.* ☎ *21-810-0340. Open Tues–Sun during museum hours.*

Centro Arte Moderna Jose Acervedo Perdigão.

Art on the underground

8 ★★★ Centro de Arte Moderna Jose Acervedo Perdigão. Part of the Calouste Gulbenkian Foundation (p 17), CAMJAP (as it's known) is in a modern building designed by José Sommer Ribeiro. Opened in 1983, it has landscaped gardens (like its sister museum round the corner), which provide an ideal setting for outdoor sculpture. The museum gives a fine overview of Portuguese and international art from 1910 onwards. Look out for works by Sonia and Robert Delaunay, Maria Helena Vieira da Silva, Arpad Szenes, and Cândido Portinari. I was also impressed by the collection of works by British artists such as Antony Gormley, and an Armenian collection, including paintings by Arshile Gorky. 🕐 *60–90 min. Rua Dr Nicolau Bettencourt.* 📞 *21-823-474. www.camjap.gulbenkian.pt. Admission 2€, combined Gulbenkian & CAMJAP 5€, free seniors & students & Sun. Open Tues–Sun 10am–6pm. Metro: São Sebastião, Praça de Espanha. Bus: 16, 26, 31, 46, 56.*

9 ★★★ Museu Nacional do Azulejo. The National Tile Museum chronologically follows the development of techniques used to make *azulejos* as well as the style and theme. Follow the changes within the tile industry here and you also begin to understand social, cultural, economic, and political history. My top picks include the early imitations of Moorish tiles for their knots and twists; 16th-century panels influenced by the Renaissance styles from Flanders, particularly the *Painel de Nossa Senhora da Vida*; an elaborate religious scene by Marçal de Matos, c1580, depicting the Virgin and other figures; and

Cherub at the Museu Nacional dos Azulejos

Museu de Artes Decorativas

from the "Cycle of the Masters," a panel by Willem van der Kloet (1666–1747), which shows aristocrats dancing on a terrace. In the 20th century António Costa's Art Deco tiles stand out for their artistic finesse, but the best modern tiles can be found in the metro. ⏱ 60–90 min. *Rua Madre de Deus.* ☎ *21-810-0340. www.mnazulejo-ipmuseus.pt. Admission 3€, 1.50€ 15–25 years, seniors, teachers, 1.20€ youth card holders. Open Tues 2pm–6pm, Wed–Sun 10am–6pm, closed Mon, Easter Sun, New Year, May 1, Dec 25. Bus: 718, 742, 794 (stop outside the museum), 25, 759 (Avenida Dom Henrique).*

⑩ ★ **Museu de Artes Decorativas.** This decorative arts museum is set in an eye-catching Alfama palace dating back to the 17th century. Inside, it's like stepping back into an 18th-century aristocrat's home, with a large collection of 18th-century furniture, textiles, tiles, porcelain and glassware. The added bonus of this museum is that it runs courses teaching traditional crafts. ⏱ *45mins-1 hour. Largo das Portas do Sol, 2;* ☎ *21 888 1991. Admission 4€, 2€ seniors/students, 3.20€ Lisboa Card, free under 12s. Open Thurs–Sun 10am–5pm.*

⑪ **Metro.** Lisbon's metro is the best place to see modern azulejos, and you can do it while on the move. My top five include: **Alto dos Moinhos** station with images of Fernando Pessoa by Julio Pomar; **Campo Grande,** a pastiche on 17th-century tiles placed in the wrong order by Eduardo Nery; the library images by Bartolomeu Cid dos Santos in **Entre Campos** station; the paintings of fruit at **Laranjeiras;** and the brightly colored abstract scenes by Yayoi-Kusama at **Oriente** (also see the contemporary panels throughout the Parque das Nações, see p 18). *Open daily 6.30am–1am.* ●

The **Alfama**

1 ★ start here

Largo da Graça
Trav. da Pereira
Graça †
Largo da Graça
GRAÇA
Rua da Verónica
R. Voz do Operario
Rua Entremuros do Mirante

MOURARIA

R. dos Cavaleiros
R. da Guia
R. da Mouraria
R.Marq.Ponte Lima
Rua das Largas
Cc. de Santo André
Trav. das Monicas
Largo Rodrigues Freitas

Campo de Sta. Clara
Arco Grande de Cima
Rua do Mirante

Castelo de São Jorge

Largo St. Vicente
Cc. de S. Vicente
Cc. do Trólo
R. dos Escolas
R. Guilh. Braga
R. dos Corvos

ALFAMA

Rua do Paraíso
Rua dos Caminhos de Ferr.

Rua da Costa do Castelo
R. Chão da Feira
R. Milagre S. Ant.
R. de S. Mamede
R. das Damas
R. Norberto de Araújo
R. do Castelo
R. de S.
R. do Salvador
R. da Regueira
R.do Limoeiro
R. da
R. Augª Rua de S. Pedro
R. dª

Largo S. Martinho
R. do Barão
R. de São João da Praça
R. T. do Trigo

16 ★ finish here

R. Afonso de Albuquerque
R. dos Bacalhoeiros
R. Cais Santarém

Av. Infante Dom Henrique

0	200 yards
0	200 metres

5 Castelo de São Jorge
6 Museu de Artes Decorativas
7 Miradouro de Santa Luzia
8 Mosteiro de São Vicente
9 Igreja de Santa Engrácia
10 Igreja de Santa Luzia e São Bras
11 Museu do Teatro Romano
12 Sé (Cathedral)
13 Igreja de Santo António
14 Clube de Fado
15 Casa dos Bicos
16 Jewish Quarter

1 Largo Martim Moniz
2 Capela de Nossa Senhora da Saúde
3 Alfama Streets
4 Treasureland

The hilly Alfama is the birthplace of the city, an ancient and crumbling neighborhood in parts, but one with a strong character and sense of community. On the way up to the castle and back down to the Baixa you'll absorb a good helping of daily life; hear women pass the gossip as they hang out the washing, discover a great little bar or fado restaurant, and spot tumbledown buildings with decorative azulejos (tiles). START: **Metro: Martim Moniz.**

---

1 Largo Martim Moniz. Exit from the metro onto this large, redeveloped square. It's actually between the Baixa and Mouraria, but a good place to start the walk as you have the option of avoiding the steep climb upwards. If you don't fancy the first part of the walk you can take tram 28 from here and either jump off at Mosteiro de São Vicente or Museu de Artes Decorativas and pick up the walk from there.

2 ★ Capela de Nossa Senhora de Saúde. This small chapel is between the left-hand side of the square (as you look towards Hotel Mundial) and Rua da Mouraria. It's dedicated to the "Virgin of Health" for having put an end to a plague in 1569. Her statue stands inside at the front of the chapel, dressed in lace with toys and personal artifacts left at her feet by devotees. As well as an elaborate wood and gold leaf altar, there are intricate panels of

tiles along the walls. ⏱ *10 min.*
Open Mon–Fri 8.45am–6pm; Sat
8.45am–1pm & 3–6pm; Sun & public
holidays 8.45am–12pm.

③ ★ **Alfama streets.** On the
same side of the square is a steep
set of steps, Escadinhas da Saúde.
Brace your muscles and climb them
to the top. Then turn right onto Rua
Marquês Ponte de Lima (don't be
surprised if local women lean out of
the windows above to chat across
the street with a neighbor) and then
left (a few more steps) and right
onto Costa do Castelo. A typical
cobbled Alfama street, here you'll
see various examples of basic (functional) tiles on the outside of the
houses. Some of the houses in the
Alfama have been here for genera-
tions, the tiles added later and
almost holding them up. They're
mass produced, rather than artistic,
serve a purpose in keeping the
weather out, and I consider them
one of the key features of the city's
streetscape. Look out for the tiled
exterior on the right with country
scenes along the top, and at a bend

Decorated streets by the castle.

Chapitô art center

in the road a fine residential property displaying blue and white tiles
with religious iconography.

Just round the bend you'll see
Chapitô, an arts center with a
restaurant (see p 131). After this the
road becomes Rua do Milagre de
Santo António, the houses various
pastel shades with the first of several tourist shops, Bilha. Turn left
into Rua Bartolomeu de Gusmão,
right at the top, and an immediate
left onto the ramp into the castle.

St George at entrance to Castelo de São Jorge.

4 ★ **Treasure Land.** Pop into this bar/restaurant as you ascend Rua Bartolomeu de Gusmão. Small and rustic, the owners are enthusiastic and speak English (one of them is Irish). Don't expect anything fancy, but it's an authentic Alfama watering hole. **A** *Rua Bartolomeu de Gusmão, 11–13.* ☎ *218 863 960. Open daily 8.30am–midnight. $$.*

5 ★★★ **Castelo de São Jorge** Enter the castle precincts through the Arco de São Jorge (Arch of St. George), which along with the castle walls marks the ancient perimeter of the fortress. The path bears right into Rua de Santa Cruz do Castelo. Santa Cruz is a small community living on a few streets within the castle walls. Other sights within the castle walls include the Casa do Governador (ticket office and shop) and, past the ticket barrier, the Prasa das Armas (large square and viewing point) and the Royal Palace (where the castle café and Casa do Leão restaurant are located), the *Castelejo* (castle towers and internal walls), and the Islamic Quarter. This is now known as the Praça Nova or New Square and archeological digs have revealed several remains of 11th- and 12th-century houses.

From outside the castle café you can spy the Solar do Castelo Heritage Hotel (p 148) through the fence opposite. Located on Rua das Cozinhas, the palace kitchens are believed to have been here. ⏱ *60 –90 min. Alfama.* ☎ *21-880-0620. www.castelosaojorge.egeac. pt. Admission 5€; 30% discount*

View of the River Tagus from Castelo de São Jorge.

Mosteiro de São Vicente de Fora has impressive interior decoration

Lisboa Card; under 10s & seniors free. Open Nov–Feb 9am–6pm; Mar–Oct 9am–9pm.

6 ★ Museu de Artes Decorativas (Museum of Decorative Arts). Housed in the 17th-century Azurara Palace, this array of period furniture, textiles, tiles, porcelain, and glassware gives an insight into the trappings of aristocratic life during the 18th century. The collection was brought together by Ricardo do Espirito Santo in the mid-20th century and was donated by him to the state. A foundation named after him runs workshops and courses here in traditional crafts. ⏱ *60–90 min. Largos das Portas do Sol, 2.* ☎ *21-888-1991. Admission 4€, 2€ seniors/students, 3.20€ Lisboa Card, free under 12s. Open Thu–Sun 10am–5pm.*

7 ★★ Miradouro de Santa Luzia and Largo das Portas do Sol. As you exit the castle grounds, follow the wall to the left along the cobbled street round to the right by the Belmonte Hotel (see p 146) and head downhill until you come to the tram tracks and the Miradouro de Santa Luzia. This viewing point is by the Igreja de Santa Luzia—see below) and to the left

the Largo das Portas do Sol as you approach from the castle. On sunny days there are tables and chairs set out where you can enjoy refreshment from the coffee booth. Note the steps on the right of the patio (Rua Norberto de Araujo)—these date back to the Moorish occupation. Looking towards the hill on the left, the large white building with two bell towers is the Mosteiro de São Vicente de Fora (monastery and church), where we're heading next. Hop on tram 28 heading towards Graça or follow the tram tracks, which zigzag along the narrow Alfama streets.

8 ★★ Mosteiro de São Vicente de Fora. The tram stops outside this monastery—you'll see the steps leading up to the large white church. It's worth paying the entrance fee to see the monastery (through the gates on the right), a "hidden" gem. Its impressive cloisters are lined with large tiled panels, and the sacristy has intricate polychrome marble inlays, an oil painting on the ceiling, and (under the floor) the tombs of two Teutonic knights who helped Dom Afonso Henriques during the *Reconquista*

(Christian reconquest) of 1147. You can also see the pantheons, choir and views of the Alfama, Tagus and Cristo Rei from the roof/bell tower. On the ground floor there is a café and you can relax under the trellises in the peaceful courtyard. ⏱ 45–60 min. Largo de São Vicente.

⑨ ★★ Igreja de Santa Engrácia e Panteão Nacional. Located behind the church and monastery, the Church of St. Engrácia was designated the National Pantheon in 1916 and houses the tombs of several Lisbon heroes (p 38), but it's also a cool retreat from the hot Lisbon sun. Large and airy, the interior is inlaid with marble and you can go up into the dome and contemplate the colors of the city beneath. Go shortly before the church closes and you might have it to yourself. ⏱ 30–45 min. Campo de Santa Clara. ☎ 21-885-4820. www.ippar.pt. Admission 2€, 1€ 15–25 years, 0.80€ student card, free Sun and public holidays, and at all times for under 15s. Open Tues–Sun 10am–5pm. Tram: 28. Bus: 9, 25, 35, 39, 46, 81, 90, 104, 105, 107.

Lisbon's 12th-Century Cathedral

⑩ ★ Igreja de Santa Luzia e São Bras. This church is dedicated to Santa Luzia, from which the nearby Miradouro de Santa Luzia takes its name. Home of the Portuguese branch of the ancient Sovereign Order of Malta, it was built in the 12th century and funded by Dom Afonso Henriques as a reward for the Order's help in reconquering the city. In 1988, a fire damaged a good part of the church including the elaborately painted ceiling. You can just about see the remaining part in the sacristy; the rest of the church has been renovated and whitewashed and the plan is to renew the ceiling décor. In front of the church is a small viewing area with "port-holes" in the wall looking down towards the river. Stop at the far end to see the large tiled panel with scenes of the city. ⏱ 10–20 min. Largo de Santa Luzia. ☎ 21-888-1303. Admission donations.

⑪ ★ Museu do Teatro Romano. This small museum (on the right before the Sé) is on the site of a Roman theatre abandoned in the 4th century and hidden from view until the late 18th century. You can see the archeological finds and see through multimedia displays what it would have been like. ⏱ 30 min. Pátio de Aljube, 5 (off Rua Augusta Rosa). ☎ 21-751-3200. Admission 2.62€, free students & children. Open Tues–Sun 10am–1pm and 2–6pm.

⑫ ★ Sé (cathedral). Lisbon's Cathedral (see also p 23) is not the religious centerpiece of the city (that is the Mosteiro dos Jerónimos; see p 75). This 12th-century Romanesque church has a simple but impressive façade framed by two towers, a vaulted ceiling, a stained glass window of St. Anthony, cloisters, and a 14th-century ambulatory chapel and

Alfama Tiles

apse. ⏱ *20–45 min. Largo da Sé. Admission free, cloisters 2.50€.*

⑬ ★ **Igreja de Santo António de Lisboa.** Dedicated in medieval times to St. Anthony, the patron saint of Lisbon, this church was rebuilt after the 1755 earthquake but displays a mixture of architectural styles. Highlights are the baroque portal, the rococo panel on the south façade, and the barrel-vaulted marble ceiling. ⏱ *10–20 min. Largo de Santo António da Sé.* ☎ *21-886-9145. Admission free. Open daily 8am–7.30pm.*

⑭ ★★★ **Clube de Fado.** Just round the corner from the Sé, this is a renowned *fado* restaurant and a good place to hear live music in the heart of the Alfama. You'll need to book ahead though, as it's a popular venue, where owner and fado guitarist Mario Pacheco usually performs himself (see p 121). *Rua São João da Praça, 94. www.clube-de-fado.com. $$$$.*

⑮ ★ **Casa dos Bicos.** Walk through to Rua dos Bacalhoeiros to see the curious House of Points. It's rarely open to the public, but worth seeing for its spiky façade. Built in 1523 by Dom Brás de Albuquerque, it's believed he was influenced by buildings seen on a trip to Italy (see page 24) ⏱ *10 mins. Rua dos Bacalhoeiros. Tram 18, 25; bus 9, 28, 35, 81, 82, 90, 746, 759, 794,*

⑯ ★ **Jewish Quarter.** Jews were an important part of the community prior to the Reconquest and small enclaves continued to exist until the *autos da fé* (executions) started in Rossio Square in the 16th century. They lived at the foot of the Alfama in the poor narrow streets, sandwiched between Rua dos Cais de Santarém and Rua de São Pedro. ⏱ *20 mins. Metro: Baixa-Chiado, tram: 15, 18, 25; bus: 2, 81, 92, 711, 713.*

Shop for postcards and souvenirs

Avenida-Parque

0	200 yards
0	200 metres

(i) Information
⊠ Post Office
Ⓜ Metro Stop

1 Praça dos Restauradores
2 Avenida da Liberdade
3 Restaurante Quebra Mar
4 Praça Marquês de Pombal
5 Parque Eduardo VII
6 Jardim Amália Rodrígues
7 Restaurante Eleven

This is a refreshing walk to do on a Sunday morning, when the squares and avenue are relatively quiet and you can enjoy a leisurely stroll along the Avenida da Liberdade and through the Parque Eduardo VII, with its formal gardens and city views. On the other hand, if you want to flash your cash in the designer stores or treat yourself to a lunch at what was at the time of writing Lisbon's only Michelin-starred restaurant, Eleven, then you're best coming during the week. START: **Praça dos Restaurandores. Tram: xx, Bus: xx.**

1 ★★ Praça dos Restauradores. Standing in this long square, you'll feel at the heart of the city as it's an easy stroll from here to the Avenida da Liberdade, Baixa, Alfama, and the Bairro Alto. Named after the restoration of power from the Spanish in 1640, the square has a monument at its center dedicated to those that fought. All across the square is a swathe of block paving with a knot-work design reminiscent of Portugal's maritime tradition. Take in the impressive architecture around you. My favorite building here is the Eden Teatro, a former theater built in the 1930s by Cassiano Branco. Today it's an apart-hotel (p 141), but retains the external Art Deco structure, friezes and signs. The striking pink building next door, Palácio Foz, is a post-earthquake palace, today

Start your walk in the Praça dos Restauradores

housing a tourist information center. Opposite is the Hard Rock Cafe. *Metro: Restauradores. Bus: 2, 9, 36, 44, 45, 90, 91, 711, 732, 746. Elevador da Lavra. Elevador da Glória (closed for repairs at time of writing).*

2 ★★ Avenida da Liberdade. Built in 1879, this avenue brought Lisbon forward into the modern age, connecting the historic downtown with the new business district. Based on the style of the Champs Elysées in Paris, it's a pleasant strolling ground with a small quiet road and a tree-lined sidewalk with cafés separate from the busy road at the center. Under the shade of the trees you'll pass various large hotels, banks, designer shops, restaurants, theaters, and early 20th-century town houses. Look out for no. 65, the birthplace of renowned Portuguese painter and sculptor Carlos Botelho (1899–1982). Further up, under a small forest of palms, a statue of Neptune sits on a bed of rocks with water pouring into a small pond below.

3 ★★ Restaurante Quebra Mar. This is one for seafood lovers, a restaurant renowned for the freshness of its produce. Expect traditional Portuguese fish dishes such as skewers of squid, grilled grouper, and barbecued sardines. Book ahead or come early to avoid disappointment. *Avenida da Liberdade, 77.* ☎ *21-346-4855. Open Mon–Sat 12pm–1am. $$$.*

If you have some cash to flash, you might want to pop into the designer stores here, including Massimo Dutti on the right, and Mont Blanc, Hugo Boss, Ermenegildo Zegna, and Loewe on the left.

I find the monument dedicated to soldiers that fought and died in the Great War deeply moving. Held up by two struggling slaves, it's topped with Liberty, who is placing a wreath on the head of a kneeling solder.

Look out for two moviehouses: the Tivoli at no. 188, a 1920s neo-classical delight where there are occasional kids' matinees and concerts; and the modernist Cinema São Jorge, opened in 1950 complete with orchestra, cinema organ, and air conditioning. The interior was remodeled and reopened in 2001. *Metro: Restauradores, Avenida, Marquês Pombal. Bus: 2, 9, 36, 44, 45, 90, 91, 711, 732, 746. Elevador da Lavra. Elevador da Glória (closed for repairs at time of writing).*

④ ★ Praça Marquês de Pombal. More of a roundabout than a square, it's often so busy with traffic that it's not easy to get to the center. But you can see the statue of Pombal looking up to the park behind.

Praça Marques de Pombal

Neptune statue on Avenida da Liberdade

Use the tunnels and pedestrian crossings to get to the park. *Metro: Marquês Pombal. Bus: 2, 9, 36, 44, 45, 90, 91, 711, 732, 746.*

⑤ ★★ Parque Eduardo VII. There's a tree-lined road on the bottom left side of the park, and if you come in July it'll be a swathe of purple flowers. The *Feira do Livro* (book fair) also takes place here then, with books for everyone in various languages. The downside is the stalls are housed in brightly colored temporary wooden huts that spoil the overall effect of the formal gardens. At any other time, you'll get a good view of the beds, bushes and paths from the top or bottom of the park. An oasis of leisure and relaxation (p 92), it has sports facilities, greenhouses of tropical plants, ducks, geese and other wildfowl, plus a lakeside restaurant/café. I enjoy the park for its layout, its bright and sunny feel, and the views from the top; on a clear day you can see all the way down the Avenida da Liberdade and even to the river.

Stop to see the Carlos Lopes Pavilion on the right-hand side of the park. Originally built in Brazil to mark the 100th anniversary of its independence in 1923, it was moved here and reconstructed in 1932. After years of hosting exhibitions and sports events, it has fallen into disrepair, disappointing considering the elaborate external *azulejos* panels depicting 18th-century style battle scenes. *Metro: Parque, Marquês Pombal. Bus: 1, 2, 11, 12, 18, 22, 23, 27, 31, 36, 42, 44, 45, 48, 51, 83, 90, 91, 113, 115, 718, 742, 746.*

6 ★★ **Jardim Amália Rodrigues.** This small garden has an intimate feel. Dedicated to *fadista* queen Amália Rodrigues (p 38), there's an eye-catching statue, Maternidad, by Colombian sculptor Fernando Botero at the entrance and across the other side of the pond a café with outdoor seating. *Alameda Cardeal Cerejeira, Alto do Parque. Open 24 hours a day. Metro: Parque. Bus: 718, 742, 746. Bus 718, 742, 746, 203.*

7 ★★★ **Restaurante Eleven.** Lisbon's only Michelin-starred restaurant at the time of writing, so you'll need to book in advance to get a table. Not the prettiest from the outside, it's the modern Portuguese cuisine inside that is prized along with the panoramic city views. *Rua Marquês de Fronteira, Jardim Amália Rodrigues.* ☎ *21-386-2211. Open Mon–Sat 12.30–3pm & 7.30–11.30pm. $$$$$.*

Purple blossom lines the edges of Parque Eduardo VII

Baixa

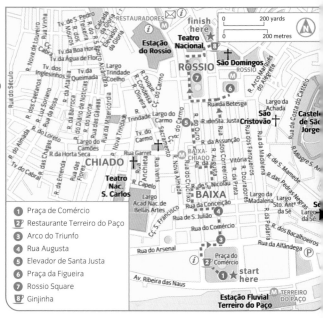

1. Praça de Comércio
2. Restaurante Terreiro do Paço
3. Arco do Triunfo
4. Rua Augusta
5. Elevador de Santa Justa
6. Praça da Figueira
7. Rossio Square
8. Ginjinha

The Baixa's grid-like layout makes it easy to navigate and a great place to get your bearings. With your back to the river, you'll see the Castelo de São Jorge and the Alfama to the right, the Chiado-Bairro Alto on the left, while straight ahead through Rossio Square leads to the Avenida da Liberdade. **START Praça do Comércio. Metro: Baixa/Chiado. Tram: 12, 15. Bus: 2, 81, 92, 711, 713.**

1 ★★ Praça do Comércio.
Whenever I visit Lisbon I always return to this bright square, where modern Lisbon began. Transformed following the world's "first modern disaster", the earthquake of 1755, the despotism and aristocratic overindulgence was put on a back burner and a new order brought to the fore. The new buildings were simple and symmetrical, facing towards each other, leaving the riverfront open to the city's lucrative mercantile business.

Today the square often hosts exciting concerts and open-air exhibitions. Look out for the main attractions: the bronze (now green) statue of Dom José I with the medallion of the Baixa's "architect", Pombal (see p 38) at the base; the Lisbon Welcome Center; the 200-year old Café Martinho da Arcada (see p 106); the Restaurante Terreiro do Paço (see p 112); and the Arco do Triunfo (see below). *Metro: Baixa-Chiado. Tram: 12, 15, 25. Bus: 2, 81, 92.*

2 ★★★ Restaurante Terreiro do Paço. Taking the square's pre-earthquake name, this restaurant is a showcase of the country's gastronomy and a good place to try regional dishes with a modern twist. *Praça de Comércio, Lisbon Welcome Center.* ☎ *21-031-2850. www. terreiropaco.com. Open Tues–Fri 12.30–3pm; 8–11pm; Sat 8–11pm. $$$$.*

3 ★★ Arco do Triunfo. The Triumph Arch links Praça do Comércio and Rua Augusta, a project that took around 100 years to complete (finished in 1873). It sports a collection of key Portuguese symbols. As well as the royal coats of arms, there are figures representing Viriato, leader of the Lusitanians who fought against Roman occupation, Nuno Alvares Pereira, general during the fight for

independence from Castille in the 14th century, explorer Vasco da Gama, and the Marquês de Pombal (see above). The Douro and Tagus rivers are also indicated, and the arch is topped with the figures of Glory, Genius, and Valor. *Praça de Comércio. Metro: Baixa-Chiado. Tram: 12, 15, 25. Bus: 2, 81, 92.*

4 ★★ Rua Augusta and the Baixa streets. This is the central shopping thoroughfare of the Baixa, and as it's pedestrianized it makes a great route to wander and watch life go by. At the bottom end there are often stalls selling prints of Lisbon and artists offering to draw your caricature. During good weather restaurants (mostly tourist oriented ones) spill onto the street.

Follow Rua Augusta all the way to Praça Pedro V (Rossio), or zigzag through the side streets, where you'll find local stores such

The Arco do Triunfo links the Praça de Comércio and Rua Augusta

Gallery on Praça do Comércio.

as Discoteca Amália (see p 89), *the place to buy* fado *music.* Note the street names, given to match the trades of the people that worked here: *ouro* (gold), *douradores* (goldsmiths), *prata* (silver), *sapateiros* (cobblers), *correeiros* (saddlers), and *fanqueiros* (drapers). *Metro: Baixa-Chiado, Rossio; Tram: 12, 15, 25, 28. Bus: 2, 9, 36, 44, 45, 81, 90, 91, 92, 711.*

⑤ ★★ **Elevador de Santa Justa.** I was astonished the first time I caught sight of this bizarre iron tower. Built by engineer Raoul Mesnier du Ponsard in 1898–1901, past rumors have claimed it was designed by Gustave Eiffel or that Ponsard was a student of his, but the former is pure hearsay and there's no proof of the latter. It's definitely worth taking a trip to the top of the lift for the view across the Baixa or to get to the Convento do Carmo, located by the upper level. 🕐 *10–20 min. Rua de Santa Justa. Admission 1.30€ with Carris travel pass; Open winter daily 7am–9pm; summer Mon–Sat 7am–11pm; Sun & public holidays 9am–11pm. Metro: Baixa-Chiado, Rossio. Tram: 15, 28. Bus: 2, 9, 36, 37, 44, 81, 92.*

⑥ ★ **Praça da Figueira.** Located east of Rossio Square, this square is the "scruffy" little brother. However, there are two renowned cafés here, Confeitaria Nacional on the south side and Pastelaria Suiça on the west (with another entrance on Rossio Square). There are also some small cheap eateries. The statue at the center of the square is Dom João I (1357–1433), but look out for the skateboarders as they can come flying across the center at a rate of knots. Head back along the south side of the square and look out for Manuel Tavares, one of Lisbon's oldest and best-stocked wine shops (see p 88). *Praça da Figueira. Metro: Baixa-Chiado, Restauradores. Tram: 12, 28. Bus: 2, 9, 36, 44, 45, 90, 91, 711.*

⑦ ★★ **Rossio Square.** This bustling space has popular cafés such as Nicola and Suiça (see p 88), bronze fountains, and stately neo-classical buildings all around.

The square wasn't always this pleasant; executions used to take place here, including the first *auto da fé* in which hundreds of people suspected of being "non-Christian" were ruthlessly slaughtered. Its

Fountain on Rossio Square.

Dom João I Statue, Praça Figueira

function changed after the 1755 earthquake, and the Inquisition building was eventually demolished to make way for the **Teatro Nacional de Dona Maria II** (see p 132).

Rossio is the square's old name; its official name today is Praça Dom Pedro IV. The **statue** on top of the pedestal was reputedly Emperor Maximilian of Mexico and rumor says it was en route to Mexico when news arrived of his assassination, so the statue ended up being passed off as a Portuguese king instead.

At the northwest end of the square is **Rossio Station** (closed for refurbishment at time of writing). Built in 1886–7 by José Luís Monteiro, it's full of elaborate neo-Manueline features such as the horseshoe-shaped doors lined with elaborate motifs, the carved figure of a knight at the center with a sword and shield, and the clock that tops the station. *Metro: Baixa-Chiado, Restauradores. Tram: 12, 28. Bus: 2, 9, 36, 44, 45, 90, 91, 711.*

8 ★★ **Ginjinha.** If you're like me, this hole-in-the-wall bar will easily become a regular aperitif stop-off during your stay. Get in line for your small, plastic cup of cherry brandy (ginjinha) and sip it with the collection of Lisboetas and visitors outside. Largo São Domingos.

Carvings on Rossio Station's façade

Cais do Sodré—Chiado—Bairro Alto

1. Mercado da Ribeira
2. Ascensor da Bica
3. Miradouro de Santa Catarina
4. Praça Luís de Camões
5. Café A Brasileira
6. Teatro Nacional de São Carlos
7. Armazens do Chiado
8. Convento do Carmo
9. Cervejaria da Trindade

I like to think of this as an 'earthy' walk, taking in the sights and sounds of everyday Lisbon life along with one of the most vibrant neighborhoods in the city. It starts in the fruit and vegetable market at Cais do Sodre and passes through the neighborhoods of Santa Catarina, Bairro Alto and Chiado, home to trendy shopping and vibrant nightlife. START: **Cais do Sodré Market. Tram: xx, Bus xx.**

1 ★★ **Mercado da Ribeira.**
You have to get the timing right for the full impact of this lively market (also referred to as Mercado 24 de Julho). Come during the afternoon and all you'll find is empty stalls and the stink of old fish as it's hosed away. It's even worth skipping breakfast to experience a slice of the action here. Come at 8am (or earlier) and you'll see stalls piled high with fresh fish and

slippery squid, as well as meat, fruit, vegetables, and flowers. You'll hear the cries of the stall-holders as they sell their goods, see Portuguese women with their checkered aprons carrying their purchases, some of them on their head. This is very much the real Lisbon. Upstairs there's a restaurant and bar, Comida da Ribeira and Ribeirarte, where you can have lunch and browse the regional

6 The Best Dining

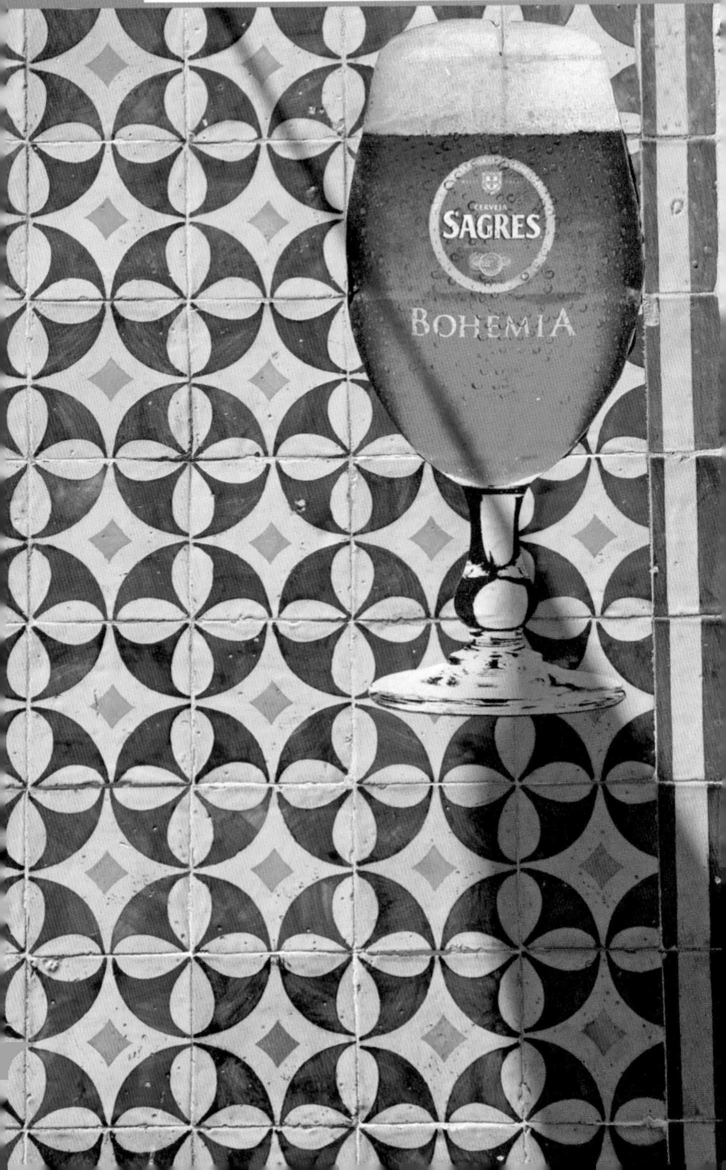

Dining Best Bets

Best **Wine List**
★★★ Nariz do Vinho Tinto $$ *Rua do Conde (p 109)*

Best **with Kids**
★★ Cervejaria Portugalia $–$$ *Avenida Brasilia, Ed. Espelho de Agua (p 107)*

Best **Celebrity Chef**
★★★ Restaurante Olivier $$$$$ *Rua do Teixeira, 35 (p 111)*

Best **Traditional Portuguese**
★★★ Belcanto $$$–$$$$ *Largo de São Carlos (p 110)*

Best **Modern Portuguese**
★★★ Alcântara Café $$$$ *Rua Maria Luisa Holstein 15 (p 105)*

Best **Fish & Seafood**
★★★ Nune's Real Marisqueira. $$$ *Rua Bartolomeu Dias (p 109)*

Best **Brazilian Rodizio (grill)**
★★ Restaurante Búfalo Grill $$$ *Rossio dos Olivais (p 110)*

Best **Cervejaria (beer hall)**
★★ Cervejaria da Trindade $$ *Rua Nova da Trindade (p 107)*

Best **Budget Dining**
★ Chimarrão $ *Armazens do Chiado (p 107)*

Best for **Cakes & Snacks**
★★★ Antiga Confeitaria de Belém $ *Rua de Belém, 84-92 (p 105)*

Best **Traditional Café**
★★ Café Martinho de Arcada $$$ *Praça do Comércio, 3 (p 106)*

Best **Literary Café**
★★ Café A Brasileira $ *Rua Garrett, 120 (p 106)*

Best **Hotel Restaurant**
★★★ Ad-Lib $$$–$$$$ *Hotel Sofitel Lisboa, Avenida da Liberdade, 127 (p 109)*

Best **City Views**
★★ Restaurante Varanda de Lisboa $$$ *Hotel Mundial, Praça Martim Moniz, 2 (p 143)*

Best for **Entertainment**
See nightlife *(p 113)*

Best **Fado Restaurant**
See nightlife *(p 113)*

Best **Riverside Restaurant**
★★ Café In $$$–$$$$ *Avenida Brasilia, Pavilhão Nascente (p 106)*

Best for **Special Occasions**
★★★ Bica do Sapato $$$ *Avenida Dom Henrique, Arm. B, Cais da Pedra (p 105)*

Best for **Romantic Dining**
★★★ Casa do Leão $$$$ *Castelo de São Jorge (p 106)*

Best **Award-Winning**
★★★ Eleven $$$$$ *Rua Marquês de Fronteira, Jardim Amália Rodrigues (p 108)*

Best **Historic Restaurant**
★★★ Tavares $$$$$ *Rua da Miseracordia (p 112)*

Dining outside, Largo do Carmo.

Tiled wall in the lively Mercado da Ribeira.

crafts on sale at A Loja de Arte-sano. Return out of the front entrance, walk round to the back of the market, strolling right through the pleasant square of Praça de São Paulo and left into Rua de São Paulo. Abruptly, away

from the bustle of the market, you find yourself in a street where faded tile-clad houses display ornate iron balconies. ⏱ *30–45 min. Avenida 24 de Julho.* ☎ *21-031-2600. [Open] Tues–Sat 5am–2pm. Tram: 15, 18, 5. Bus: 6, 35, 36, 40, 44, 45, 58, 82, 91.*

❷ ★ **Ascensor da Bica.** Keep your eyes peeled for the entrance to the elevator as it's easy to walk straight past. Buy your ticket from the man at the door and find yourself a seat onboard the small funicular train, or least something to hold onto. It's a steep ride but great to be able to look out of the back window for a bird's-eye view of the neighborhood. The funicular slides up to the Bairro Alto, passing narrow residential streets and alleyways. It's good to get your feet back on firm ground as you really feel the pull downwards. ⏱ *5–10 min. Largo da Calhariz, Rua de São Paulo. Admission 1.30€ or free with Carris travel pass. Open Mon–Sat 7am–9pm; Sun & public holidays 9am–9pm.*

Climb onboard the funicular.

Statue of Fernando Pessoa outside the Café A Brasileira

③ ★ **Miradouro de Santa Catarina.** Turn left out of the train entrance and left onto Rua Mal Saldanha to the *miradouro* (viewing point). This one has a balcony and plenty of shade, placed here so residents of the former palace behind could have clear sight of the waterfront. Today the palace is being transformed into the home of MuDe, the new design and fashion museum (p 49) and the viewing point is often a favorite spot for the young, "alternative" crowd. Return back to Largo de Calharis and back past the Bica elevator. *Tram: 28. Bus: 92.*

④ ★ **Praça Luís de Camões.** Further along is a small square, where cars and trams criss-cross their way from the Bairro Alto to Estrela or down to the river. There are a few trendy fashion stores here, such as Diesel. Don't forget the statue at the center of the square;

it represents Luis de Camões, the square's namesake and one of Portugal's greatest writers (p 39). *Tram: 28. Bus: 92.*

⑤ ★★ **Café A Brasileira.** Crowds gather on the wide pavement by this café just to have their photo taken with the bronze statue of modernist writer Fernando Pessoa. Maybe that's why the waiters have a reputation for their rudeness, as many don't buy a thing. This wasn't my experience, as a waiter chatted to me inside and told me I was sitting at the table where artists and writers meet daily. And downstairs in the wood-paneled dining room you can lunch well on decent Portuguese cuisine. *Rua Garrett, 120.* ☎ *21-834-6. $–$$.*

⑥ ★★ **Teatro Nacional São Carlos.** Fronting onto a large and airy square with a café spilling out beside it, São Carlos Theater is a simple neo-classical combination of white brick archways and yellow painted walls above. Inside the auditorium is a rococo gem with a lavish royal box, but if you want to see it you'll have to buy a ticket to a performance (p 129). *Rua Serpa Pinto, 9.* ☎ *21-325-3045. www.saocarlos.pt. Tram: 28. Bus: 92.*

⑦ ★★ **Armazens do Chiado.** Rebuilt along much of the area following a disastrous fire in 1988, this is a modern shopping center with high-street stores and a large FNAC (p 84). There's also a selection of eateries here—try Chimarrão for cheap, all-you-can eat Brazilian (p 107). *Rua do Carmo.* ☎ *21-390-6060. www.armazensdochiado.com. Open daily 10am–10pm (restaurants 11pm). $–$$$.*

today housing a small archaeological museum and a monument to the devastation caused by what is considered Europe's "first modern disaster". On a bright, hot Lisbon afternoon I found it poignant and eerily quiet. I sat on the steps with other visitors and contemplated the impact the earthquake had on thousands of ordinary people. ⏱ *30–60 min. Largo do Carmo. Metro: Baixa-Chiado. Tram: 28. Bus: 58, 790. Elevador de Santa Justa. Admission. Open May–Sep daily 10am–6pm, Oct–Apr daily 10am–5pm.*

Cervejaria da Trindade

⑧ ★★★ **Convento do Carmo e Museu Arqueológico.** With its elevated position looking across the Baixa, you can see the Carmo Convent from many an angle, including the Castelo de São Jorge (see p 8). It is the roof, or lack of it, that is most apparent from afar, but inside you realize the walls are still standing. It could have been totally demolished or reconstructed, but it was kept,

⑨ ★★ **Cervejaria da Trindade.** An old favorite, this is a comfortable place for a beer, meal for two, or group dining on long refectory-style tables. In fact that's what it was in a former life; a monk's dining room, reflected in the tiles at the back of the room. Go for surf 'n' turf Portuguese style or the daily specials. *Rua Nova da Trindade, 20C.* ☎ *21-342-3506. www.cervejariatrindade.com. Open daily 10am–2am (closed public holidays). $$.*

Teatro Nacional São Carlos

Belém

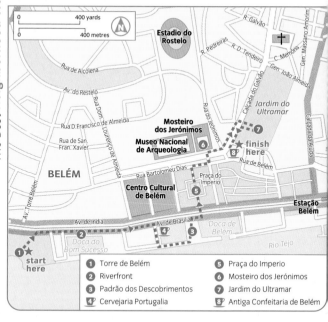

① Torre de Belém	⑤ Praça do Imperio
② Riverfront	⑥ Mosteiro dos Jerónimos
③ Padrão dos Descobrimentos	⑦ Jardim do Ultramar
④☕ Cervejaria Portugalia	⑧☕ Antiga Confeitaria de Belém

I never tire of visiting Belém with its sense of space and
light, tree-lined squares and parks—the sun reflecting from
the river onto the light-colored stone of its numerous attractions.
Not even the railway line and busy Avenida de Brasília detract from
the feel. This tour encapsulates the cream of it and visits a couple
of my favorite local eateries as well as an extra-quiet corner. START:
Tram stop: 15.

① ★★★ kids **Torre de Belém.**
Away from the busy Avenida de
Brasília (crossed by a bridge near
the tram stop), the mood becomes
more tranquil as you stroll through a
tree-shaded park. The Belém Tower
is on the other side of the park, an
island-like monument with castellated battlements. I like to sit on the
curved steps where the water gently laps up.

The Torre de Belém was built
under the orders of Dom Manuel I in

1515 as a fortress to guard the city,
a role it held until 1580, when it
became a prison under Spanish control. It continued to hold political
prisoners after Restoration in 1640
and later became a customs house.
It was declared a UNESCO World
Heritage Site (along with the
Mosteiro dos Jerónimos) in 1983.

Take in the Manueline details of
the tower (see p 14 and p 28) from
the external carved ropes and
crosses to the animal heads and
heraldic motifs. In the cellars the

damp and dark bring to life the grim reality of being imprisoned here.

🕐 30–45 min. Avenida de Brasília. ☎ 21-362-0034. www.mosteiro jeronimos.pt/index_torre.html. Admission 3€, 1.50€ 4–15 years & seniors, 1.20€ youth card holders; free under 14s, general public Sun & public holidays until 2pm. Open Oct–Apr Tues–Sun 10am–5pm, May–Sep Tues–Sun 10am–6.30pm. Train: Belém. Tram: 15. Bus: 27, 28, 29, 43, 49, 51, 112.

② ★ **River front.** Look out for the seaplane to the left of the tower, a replica of the Fairey III-B biplane Santa Cruz flown across the Atlantic in 1922. A path leads back towards the road, past the souvenir stalls. Turn right at the end.

(It was quite awkward walking between the Torre and the Discoveries Monument at the time of writing as there were large construction works going on.) You'll see waterfront restaurants such as Portugalia

Padrão dos Descobrimentos

and Ja Sei, where you can have a direct view of the Padrão dos Descobrimentos.

③ ★★★ **Padrão dos Descobrimentos.** Carefully crafted characters line this monument, made in the shape of a *caravela* boat—the

Take in the Manueline details on the Torre de Belém

Portugália Restaurant on the river front

type the explorers sailed during the 15th–16th centuries. Look out for depictions of explorers as well as royalty, mathematicians, writers, and artists. Benches on either side of the monument let you sit and take in the view of the river. Beyond you can hear the "clink-clink" of yachts moored at the marina.
🕐 10–30 min. Avenida de Brasília. ☎ 21-303-1950. Admission to viewing platform and exhibitions 2.50€, 1.50€ 7–8 years, students under 25, seniors, 30% discount Lisboa Card. Open Oct–Apr Tues–Sun 10am–6pm, May–Sep Tues–Sun 10am–7pm. Train: Belém. Tram: 15. Bus: 27, 28, 29, 43, 49, 51, 112.

Doca de Belém

☕ ★ **Cervejaria Portugália.** Part of a chain, this restaurant offers decent Portuguese cuisine at reasonable prices. This restaurant has a prime waterfront position with a terrace facing the Padrão. You can't miss it—it's bright and white and looks like it's perched on the water. *Avenida Brasilia, Edificio Espelho de Agua.* ☎ *21-303-2700. www.portugalia.pt. Open daily 12pm–1am. $$–$$$.*

⑤ ★ Praça do Império. From the Padrão, head towards the road and go through the tunnel to cross the road to the square. On hot days there's often a mobile ice-cream seller here. Then stroll through the square, where there are cypress and olive trees, and Portuguese-style black-and-white stone pathways that lead past grand, central fountains. To your left you'll see the angular modernity of Centro Cultural de Belém (p 14), contrasting with the elaborate detail of the 15th-century Mosteiro dos Jerónimos ahead.

Enjoy the tranquil cloisters at Mosteiro dos Jerónimos

6 ★★★ Mosteiro dos Jeróni-mos.

Cross the road to the monastery, where you'll find good photo opportunities, particularly the church's south portal with its intricate Manueline detail of this doorway. The main entrance is accessed via an archway (p 12). If you go at lunchtime, it should be quiet enough to take in the carved tombs, columns, chapels, and vaulted ceiling in relative peace. Don't miss out on the exquisitely tranquil cloisters, also best in the afternoon, when the sunlight filters down into the courtyard. ⏱ *60–90 min. Praça do Império.* ☎ *21-362-0034. www. mosteirojeronimos.pt. Admission cloisters 4.50€, 2.25€ 4–15 years & seniors, 1.80€ youth card holders, free under 14s, general public Sun & public holidays until 2pm. Open Oct–Apr Tues–Sun 10am–5pm, May–Sept Tues–Sun 10am–6.30pm. Train: Belém. Tram: 15. Bus: 27, 28, 29, 43, 49, 51, 112.*

7 ★★ Jardim do Ultramar.

Turn left out of the monastery and cross the square to the gateway to the right of the period property. This is a side entrance into the Ultramar Garden, also known as the Jardim-Museu Agrícola Tropical, home to some rare tropical trees and plants, and two avenues of palms that will lead you back and forth across the park. The park backs onto the Palácio de Belém, a former royal palace now home to the President of the Republic: you can't go in the palace but you can sneak a peek of its pink façade through the trees. ⏱ *20–30 min. Calçada do Galvão.* ☎ *21-362-0210. Open May–Oct Tues–Fri 10am–5pm, Sat & Sun 11am–6pm, Nov–Apr Tues–Sun 10am–5pm. Train: Belém. Tram: 15. Bus: 27, 28, 29, 43, 49, 51, 112.*

8 ★★★ Antiga Confeitaria de Belém.

For me no trip to Belém is complete without stopping off at this historic café. What's more it's right by the tram stop. Take in its wall cases of vintage port and souvenir hats, its curved bar and blue-and-white tiled walls. But most of all, complete your day with one of its famed pastries, the *pastel de Belém,* a custard tart that is great accompaniment to a *meia de leite* (coffee with milk). *Rua de Belém, 84-92.* ☎ *21-363-7423.*

Enjoy local pastries at Antiga Confeitaria de Belém

Rato—Bairro Alto

- **1** Largo do Rato
- **2** Synagogue
- **3** Parque das Amoreiras
- **4** Real Fabrica
- **5** Jardim Botânico
- **6** Rua da Escola Politécnica
- **7** Praça do Principe Real
- **8** Miradouro de São Pedro de Alcântara

This is a diverse walk, with a little sightseeing and as much shopping as you wish. It passes through an eclectic neighborhood from the busy junction of Largo do Rato, uphill to the aqueduct then down again to finish at the Miradouro de São Pedro de Alcântara. En route, you'll see a synagogue, delis and cafés, carpet makers and second-hand bookstores as well as a couple of parks.
START: **Metro: Rato. Bus: 6, 9, 58, 74.**

1 ★ **Largo do Rato.** This square is a departure point, not just for the metro station underneath (check out the abstract *azulejos* panels by Arpad Szènés and Vieira da Silva) and the bus station at its center, but also because of the various roads that lead off it. Around the edge are inexpensive eateries, popular with locals and rarely frequented by tourists. Walk round to the top of Rua Alexandre Herculano and you can delve into the Charcutaria Brasil for an even cheaper packed lunch of fresh

cheese, ham and bread. *Largo do Rato. Metro: Rato. Bus: 6, 9, 58, 74.*

2 ★ **Synagogue.** A rare find in Portugal, this early 20th-century synagogue is called *Shaaré TiKvà* in Hebrew, which in English means Doors of Hope. You have to call ahead to go inside but you can attend Friday and Saturday worship. The Inquisition was only abolished in 1821 and until this synagogue was built, the Jewish population worshipped in small apartments. *Rua Alexandre*

Herculano, 59. ☎ 21-385-8604. *Worship winter Fri 7pm, summer Fri 8pm, Sat 9am (subject to alteration). Metro: Rato. Bus: 6, 9, 58, 74.*

3 ★★ Parque das Amoreiras. This park was named after the mulberry trees once planted here to feed the silk worms at the nearby factory, now long gone. Small and compact, part of the city's aqueduct towers above and down below are 18th-century *azulejos* panels by António Oliveira Bandeiras. *Praça das Amoreiras. Open 24 hours a day. Metro: Rato. Bus: 58, 74.*

18th-century azulejos panels in the Parque das Amoreiras

4 ★★ Real Fabrica. Located on the south side of Rato, on the corner of Rua da Escola Politécnica, this café is a good marker to check you're going down the right street. A former silk factory (see above), it's also a quiet place to stop for a *meia de leite* (coffee with milk) or *galão* (milky coffee in a glass) and a custard-filled pastry. *Rua da Escola Politécnica. ☎ 21-385-2090.*

5 ★★ Jardim Botanico. Great for escaping a hectic city day, there's plenty to explore here. Don't miss the herb house by the entrance or the butterflies with hundreds of monarchs and pupae waiting to hatch. Cool off in the shade and catch a view through trees over the city. *Rua da Escola Politécnica, 58. ☎ 21-392-1800. www.jb.ul.pt. Admission 1.50€,; 0.75€ seniors, students, youth card holders; free under 6s. Metro: Rato.*

6 ★ Rua da Escola Politécnica. This street is a mixture of science, learning, arts, crafts and shopping. Next to the Botanic Gardens are the Science and Natural History museums, and opposite is

Explore the shops around Rato

The Jardim Botânico has a compact and colorful butterfly house.

the Casa dos Tapetes de Arraiolos, a carpet shop with a difference—you can buy a kit to make your own (see p 86). Further down the street you'll see a theatre (Teatro Politecnica), antique shops and second-hand book stores, time for you to have a rummage for that elusive tome. *Rua da Escola Politécnica, 58. Metro: Rato. Bus: 58, 790.*

❼ ★ Praça do Principe Real. Like the rest of the street, this park has a little of everything: two cafés, a play area for kids, an underground water museum at the center and plenty of shade. At night it is a popular hang-out for the gay community. *Praça do Principe Real. Admission free. Open 24 hours a day. Bus: 58, 790.*

❽ ★ Miradouro de São Pedro de Alcântara. A perfect place to finish your walk. This wide *miradouro* has recently had a major makeover, extending it downwards to make a mini bedded park, maximizing its balcony view across the city. This is the

place to take pictures, peer across to the hill opposite, where the Castelo de São Jorge crowns the Alfama and makes a spectacular view. *Rua Dom Pedro V. Metro: Restauradores. Elevador da Glória (closed for repairs at time of writing).* ●

Take in the spectacular view from the Miradouro

Shopping Best Bets

Best Bric-à-Brac Market
★★★ Feira da Ladra, *Campo de Santa Clara (p 84)*

Best Wine Shop
★★★ Manuel Tavares, *Rua da Batesga, 1A-B (p 88)*

Best Leather Goods
★★★ Loewe, *Avenida da Liberdade, 185 (p 90)*

Best Azulejos (tiles)
★★★ Fabrica de Sant'Ana, *Rua do Alecrim, 96 (p 85)*

Best Lisbon Souvenirs ★★ Artesanato do Tejo, *Rua do Arsenal, 25*

Best Antiques
★★★ Muteira Antiguidades, *Rua Augusta Rosa (p 84)*

Best Street Shopping
★★ Baixa, *Rua Augusta (p 86)*

Best Designer Shopping
★★ Avenida da Liberdade and Rua do Carmo *(p 86)*

Best Art Gallery
★ Galeria Pedro Serrenho, *Rua Almeida e Sousa, 21A (p 84)*

Best Department Store
El Corte Inglés, *Between Avenidas Antonio Augusto e Aguiar and Marquês da Fronteira e Sidónio Pais (p 85)*

Best Mall for Kids
★★ Vasco da Gama shopping center, *Parque das Nações (p 86)*

Best Jewelry
★★ Augusta Joalheiros, *Rua Augusta, 106-8 (p 89)*

Best Portuguese Designer Store
★★★ Ana Salazar, *Rua do Carmo, 87 (p 87)*

Best Shoe Shop
★★ Leninha, *Avenida Ressano Garcia, 11-D (p 90)*

Best Hat Shop
★★ Azevedo Rua, *Dom Pedro IV, 72-73 (p 87)*

Souvenir shop in the Alfama.

City Center Shopping

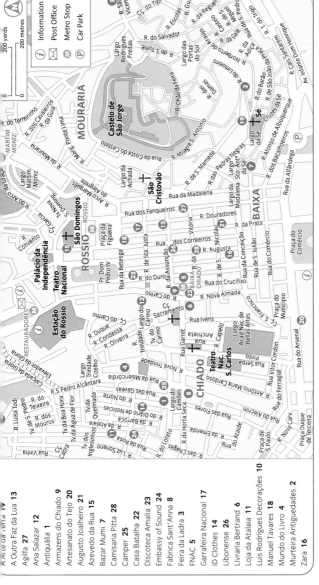

North of Center Shopping

Lisbon **Shopping A to Z**

Antiques & Art

★ **Antiquália** BAIRRO ALTO   This store stocks some choice pieces of furniture, much of it from the Far East, as well as a good variety of lighting, porcelain, and ceramics. *Praça Luís de Camões, 37.* ☎ *21-342-3260. AE, DC, MC, V. Tram: 28. Map p 81.*

★★ **M. Muteira Antiguidades** ALFAMA   Pieces range from 15th-century sculptures and 17th-century furniture to 20th-century fine art. These are investment pieces so don't call in unless you're really serious. *Rua Augusta Rosa.* ☎ *21-886-3851. www.murteira-antiguidades.com. AE, DC, MC, V. Tram: 12, 28. Map p 81.*

★ **Feira da Ladra** ALFAMA Come here early on a Tuesday or Saturday morning to rummage among the stalls. As they say, what's one man's rubbish is another's gold, so you might find that elusive old accordion you were looking for to take home. *Campo de Santa Clara. Tram: 12, 28. Map p 81.*

★ **Galeria Pedro Serrenho** CAMPO DE OURIQUE   A bright and

Have a good rummage at the Feira da Ladra.

modern gallery with a collection of contemporary fine art works by Portuguese and international artists, many of them abstract but all very different in style. *Rua Almeida e Sousa, 21A.* ☎ *21-393-0714. www.galeriapedroserrenho.com. AE, MC, V. Metro: Rato. Map p 82.*

Books

★★ **Mundo do Livro** BAIRRO ALTO   A veritable treasure trove of out-of-print books in various languages, along with ancient maps and authentic and reproduction prints. They'll also mount and frame them according to your specifications. *Largo da Trindade, 12.* ☎ *21-346-9951. www.mlivro.pt. AE, MC, V. Metro: Rossio. Map p 81.*

★★ **FNAC** BAIXA/CHIADO   FNAC is a large and reliable store for books, including some in English, as well as music, electronics and concert tickets. You can even pick up a book and browse through it in the café. As well as the Baixa, you'll find stores in most of the large shopping centers. *Armázens do Chiado, Rua do Carmo, 2.* ☎ *707-313-435. www.fnac.pt. AE, MC, V. Metro: Baixa-Chiado. Map p 81.*

★ **Livraria Bertrand** BELEM Bertrand is a chain with stores in just about every shopping center, plus Bairro Alto and the Belém Cultural Center. There's a wide selection of subjects, with some in English. *Rua Garrett, 17.* ☎ *21-347-6122. AE, DC, MC, V. Metro: Baixa-Chiado. Map p 81. CCB, Praça do Imperio.* ☎ *21-364-5637. AE, DC, MC, V. Tram: 15. Picoas Plaza, Rua Tomás Ribeiro.* ☎ *21-359-3359. AE, DC, MC, V. Metro: Picoas, Parque. Map p 82.*

Ceramics, Pottery & Tiles

★★ Bazar Mumi ALFAMA This store next to the cathedral sells genuine hand-painted tiles. You can usually see the artists at work and they also make pieces to individual specifications. *Largo de Santo António da Sé.* ☎ *21-887-0089. AE, DC, MC, V. Tram: 28. Map p 81.*

★★★ Fabrica Sant'Anna BAIRRO ALTO Simply the best place to buy tiles to take home. They're all hand-made and absolutely exquisite, from the functional style to elaborate panels covered in still life or pastoral scenes; also ceramic pots, vases and basins. You can visit the factory or even take a class yourself, but phone first. *Rua do Alecrim, 96.* ☎ *21-342-2537. www.fabrica-santanna.com. MC, V. Metro: Baixa-Chiado. Map p 81.*

Factory and 2nd showroom: *Calçada da Boa-Hora, 96.* ☎ *21-363-292. MC, V. Tram: 15.*

Department Stores/ Shopping Centers

★★ Amoreiras Shopping AMOREIRAS Between the business district and Campo de Ourique, this shopping center is housed in an

The eye-catching Amorieras Shopping Centre.

Armázens do Chiado

eye-catching modern mirrored building. The mall has 275 shops, including Habitat, Macmoda and Pão de Açucar supermarket, plus a multiplex cinema and international chains. There's also a Zara opposite the entrance. *Avenida Engenheiro Duarte Pacheco.* ☎ *21-381-0200. www.amoreiras.com. Metro: Rato, Pombal. Map p 82.*

★★ Armázens do Chiado CHIADO This compact shopping center has 41 stores from FNAC to Adolfo Dominguez, plus 11 restaurants. In the heart of the city, you can enter via the ground floor in the Baixa and exit in the Chiado. *Rua do Carmo.* ☎ *21-321-0600. www.armazensdochiado. com. Metro: Baixa-Chiado. Map p 81.*

★★★ Centro Colombo LUZ The largest shopping center in the Iberian peninsula, it boasts more than 420 shops, a supermarket, 60 restaurants, a multiplex cinema with 10 screens, amusements, and a health club. *Avenida Lusiada.* ☎ *21-711-3600. Metro: Colegio Militar.*

★★ El Corte Inglés PARQUE Spain's largest department store found its way to Lisbon a few years ago. Everything from fashion and

Best Shopping Areas

Lisbon's **Baixa** district is a traditional shopping area with international chains and home-grown leather and jewelry stores. On Rua de Ouro, some stores link to the **Chiado** and its compact mall, Armazens do Chiado. Along Rua do Carmo and Rua Garrett are international and local designer stores, but for high-end designer fashion, browse the **Avenida da Liberdade.** In **Saldanha**, you'll find the quality Spanish department store El Corte Inglés, along with other small renowned stores all the way up to **Campo Grande**. For antiques, rugs and second-hand books, start at **Rato** and stroll along Rua de São Bento or Rua da Escola Politécnica towards the Bairro Alto. Rummage for bargains at the Feira da Ladra market in the **Alfama** on Tuesdays and Saturdays. For large shopping malls, make a bee-line for **Amoreiras Shopping,** near Rato, take the metro to **Oriente** for Vasco da Gama Shopping or **Colégio Militar** for Colombo Shopping.

furnishings to a supermarket and restaurant, and you could spend the whole day here. *Between Avenidas Antonio Augusto e Aguiar and Marquês da Fronteira e Sidónio Pais.* ☎ *21-371-1700. www.elcorte ingles.pt. AE, DC, MC, V. Metro: São Sebastião. Map p 82.*

★★ Vasco da Gama Shopping

PARQUE DAS NACOES   Lisbon's newest mall at the time of writing, an attractive, large glass building by

The Vasco da Gama shopping experience

Oriente train station and leading out into the Parque das Nações. It has around 120 stores, a supermarket, 36 restaurants, a 10-screen cinema, health club and a kids' play area. *Avenida Dom João II.* ☎ *1-893-0600. www.centrovascodagama.com. Metro: Oriente. Map p 16.*

Designer Home Goods & Furnishings

★★ Agilfa BAIXA   There's everything from fine crystal glassware and porcelain to cooking utensils and cutlery at this Portuguese store. *Rua dos Fanqueiros, 226-232.* ☎ *91-739-1532. www.algifa.pt. AE, DC, MC, V. Metro: Baixa-Chiado. Map p 81.*

★★★ Casa dos Tapetes de Arraiolos BAIRRO ALTO   For the past couple of decades this company has been making rugs and tapestries, some with an antique style. You can buy them ready made from this store or in kit form and make your own. *Rua da Imprensa Nacional, 116E.* ☎ *21-396-3354. www.casatapetesarroiolos.com. AE, DC, MC, V. Tram: 28. Map p 82.*

Check out A Outra Face da Lua for quality vintage clothes and accessories.

★ **Luís Rodrígues Decorações**
BAIRRO ALTO   If you like Portuguese elegance, you can find everything you need here to furnish a house or apartment from carpets and pieces of furniture to complete interior design. *Rua Dom Pedro V, 84.* ☎ *21-346-8836. lrdeco.com. AE, DC, MC, V. Metro: Rossio, Restauradores. Map p 81.*

★ **Loja da Atalaia** BAIRRO ALTO
This store is renowned for its immaculate and stylish retro furniture, mostly from the 1950s to the 1980s. You might pick out something difficult to find back home. *Rua da Atalaia, 71.* ☎ *21-346-2093. AE, DC, MC, V. Tram: 28. Map p 81.*

Fashion & Accessories
★★★ **Ana Salazar** CHIADO   Ana Salazar has been making waves in the Portuguese fashion industry since the 1970s. Her designs are still at the forefront of cutting-edge design. Be prepared to splash out if you want quirky pieces from her latest collections. *Rua do Carmo, 87.* ☎ *21-347-2289. www.anasalazar.pt. AE, MC, V. Metro: Baixa-Chiado. Map p 81.*

★★★ **A Outra Face da Lua**
BAIXA/ALFAMA   An Aladdin's cave of vintage finds from 1920s flapper dresses to disco chic. Designer Carla

Belchior also sells her recycled clothing here, new styles created out of fashion fauxs. Take a look at the oddly placed but interesting collection of tin toys and wallpaper. *Rua da Assunção, 22.* ☎ *21-886-3430. MC, V. Metro: Baixa-Chiado. Map p 81. Alfama store: Calçada do Correio Velho, 7.* ☎ *21-886-3186. AE, DC, MC, V. Tram: 28.*

★★ **Camisaria Pitta** BAIXA
This is one of Lisbon's oldest shirt shops (for men), with attentive shop assistants who will help you find whatever style you need. They also do alterations and tailor-made suits. *Rua Augusta, 195.* ☎ *21-342-7526. AE,DC, MC, V. Metro: Baxia-Chiado. Map p 81.*

★ **Gant Flagshipstore** AVENIDA
To get the American polo and sailing-set look, head to Gant in Avenida da Liberdade. It's all very smart-casual from sport jumpers with badges and logos to scarves, ties and footwear. *Avenida da Liberdade, 38.* ☎ *21-343-3276. AE, DC, MC, V. Metro: Restauradores, Avenida. Map p 82.*

★ **Azevedo Rua Lda** BAIXA
This shop on Rossio Square has a traditional wooden shop front with a variety of hats displayed in the window. It's the kind of store frequented

Traditional hat shop on Azevedo Rua

by elegant gentlemen all their lives but the younger generation shouldn't bypass it as there's plenty of wearable caps and berets here for the fashion conscious. *Praça Dom Pedro IV, 72-73.* ☎ *21-347-0817. AE, MC, V. Metro: Rossio. Map p 81.*

★ **ID Clothes** BAIRRO ALTO This home-grown store, started up north in Porto, will appeal to the trendy young things. You'll find everything from the latest 1940s style dresses to sparkly silver disco numbers, with bags and shoes to match, of course. *Rua dos Salgadeiros, 10.* ☎ *21-347-7102. AE, MC, V. Tram: 28. Map p 81.*

★ **Zara** BAIXA PARQUE These days no city (or lady's wardrobe) would be complete without Zara. Relatively cheap and cheerful, it has all your basic tops to suits, evening-wear, shoes and accessories. Also has branches in all the main shopping areas and malls. *Rua Augusta, 71-81.* ☎ *21-324-1400. AE, DC, MC, V. Metro: Baixa-Chiado. Map p 81. Other location: Avenida António Aguiar, 134.* ☎ *21-312-9690. Metro: Parque, São Sebastião.*

Gourmet Food & Drink
★ **Charcutaria Brasil** RATO A little off the tourist trail, this store is

tellingly used widely by the locals. You'll find everything for a picnic from tasty *presunto* (cured meat), goat's cheese, freshly cooked chicken from the spit and fresh fruit to bottles of water and wine. *Rua Alexandre Herculano, 90.* ☎ *21-388-5644. AE, DC, MC, V. Metro: Rato. Map p 82.*

★★ **Garrafeira Nacional** BAIXA A good range of national and international wines as well as fortified wines such as port and Madeira, and spirits such as *aguardente* (fire water). *Rua de Santa Justa, 18.* ☎ *21-887-9080. MC, V. Metro: Baixa-Chiado. Map p 81.*

★★ **Manuel Tavares Lda** BAIXA One of the city's oldest stores, and with a traditional wood-framed shop front, it has select Portuguese wines and international liquors, as well as *chouriços*, meats and cheeses from the delicatessen, colorful displays of glacé fruits and mouthwatering chocolates. *Rua da Batesga, 1A-B.* ☎ *21-342-4209. www.manueltavares.com. AE, DC, MC, V. Metro: Rossio. Map p 81.*

Gifts
★★ **A Arte da Terra** ALFAMA Located in a historic building with vaulted ceilings, right in the heart of the Alfama, this store prides itself on selling some of the best samples of regional crafts from decorated tiles to paintings of Lisbon. *Rua de Augusto Rosa.* ☎ *21-274-5975. AE, MC, V. Tram: 28. Map p 81.*

★ **Artesanato do Tejo** BAIXA Part of the Lisbon Welcome Center, this handicraft shop is located round the corner in Rua Arsenal. It sells Lisbon-themed t-shirts, tiles, jewelry made by local artists, *fado* CDs and tourist guides. *Rua do Arsenal, 25.* ☎ *21-031-2820. AE, MC, DC, MC, V. Metro: Baixa-Chiado. Map p 81.*

★★ Linho Bordado SALDANHA
A little off the main tourist route, but worth a visit for its traditional handmade lace and embroidery. It's not cheap but there are pieces for most budgets from bread basket liners to sheets. *Ria Cidade da Horta, 36A.* ☎ *21-314-0279. AE, MC, V. Metro: Saldanha, Arroios. Map p 82.*

Jewelry
★★ Augusto Joalheiro BAIXA
This traditional jewelry shop is on the Baixa's busiest street. As well as silver and gold jewelry, it sells quality watches and silverware. *Rua Augusta, 106-8.* ☎ *21-346-0616. AE, DC, MC, V. Metro: Baixa-Chiado. Map p 81.*

Casa Batalha CHIADO   This family-run jewelry store has been in business since the 17th century. Expect quality goods and a personal service. They also have a store in Amoreiras shopping center. *Armazens do Chiado.* ☎ *21-342-7313. AE, DC, MC, V. Metro: Baixa-Chiado. Other branch: Shopping Amoreiras.* ☎ *21-691-8912. Map p 81.*

Fado Recordings

Music
★★★ Discoteca Amália BAIXA
If you want to take some *fado* music home with you, then there's no better place than this store. Named after the diva of all *fadistas*, Amália Rodrigues, it has both traditional and modern recordings. You can always ask at the counter for advice. *Rua Aurea, 274.* ☎ *21-342-1485. MC, V. Metro: Baixa-Chiado. Map p 81.*

★★ Embassy of Sound BAIRRO ALTO   A real treat for reggae lovers,

The Shopping Fine Print

Portugal isn't as strict over its traditional shopping hours as its neighbor, Spain, but some stores do still close for a couple of hours at lunchtime, usually from 1pm–3pm. The upside is most shops stay open until 8pm or 9pm. In the shopping centers, you can shop any day from 10am till midnight. Markets tend to open around breakfast time or earlier and close around lunchtime.

The tourist office offer a Shopping Card, which you can purchase from any of their outlets for 3.70€ for 24 hours or 5.80€ for 72 hours. It offers discounts of between 5% and 15% at around 200 stores in the Baixa, Chiado and Avenida da Liberdade. See www.ask melisboa.com for more information.

For information on sales tax and related rebates for non E.U. residents, see p 171.

The Best Shopping

this record store is a friendly den of vinyl, CDs, and information. You can also buy concert tickets here. *Rua da Atalaia, 17.* ☎ *21-347-8017. MC, V. Tram: 28. Map p 81.*

FNAC See books.

Shoes & Leather Goods

★★ **Camper** EL BAIRRO ALTO Camper shoes have become renowned in the past decade for their distinctive curved soles, cool round toes and range of colors. *Praça Luis de Camões.* ☎ *21-342-1178. AE, DC, MC, V. Tram: 28. Map p 81.*

★★ **Charles** BAIXA   A Portuguese chain of leather stores (there are eight in Lisbon alone), where you'll find quality leather clothing for men and women, as well as a wide selection of accessories such as bags and shoes. These stores also have a more affordable range if your budget won't take it. *Rua Augusta 275-A.* ☎ *21-342-0700. AE, MC, V. Metro: Baixa Chiado.*
     Rua Augusta 109. ☎ *21-347-7360. AE, MC, V. Metro: Baixa Chiado.*
     Rua do Carmo, 105. ☎ *21-342-5500. AE, MC, V. Metro: Baixa Chiado.*

★★ **Libonense** BAIXA   This is an old-fashioned shoe shop, the kind where you get personal attention and quality leather footwear. The footwear is as classic as the shop with shoes for men, women, and children. *Rua Augusta 202-204.* ☎ *21-342-6712. AE, MC, V. Metro: Baixa Chiado. Map p 81.*

★★★ **Loewe** AVENIDA   A Spanish store that sells luxury leather goods and fashion. Located on the ground floor of the Tivoli Hotel—and you should expect to pay for the quality. *Avenida da Liberdade, 185.* ☎ *21-354-0050. AE, DC, MC, V. Metro: Avenida. Map p 82.*

★★★ **Leninha** SALDANHA   Just a short walk from the Gulbenkian Museum, this is more than a shoe shop. As well as various brands of shoes for both men and women it stocks a few fine lines in handbags, briefcases, and gloves. *Avenida Ressano Garcia, 11-D.* ☎ *21-387-7947. AE, DC, MC, V. Metro: Saldanha, Praça de Espanha. Map p 82.* ●

Souvenirs such as postcards and handicrafts can be found easily.

Parque Eduardo VII

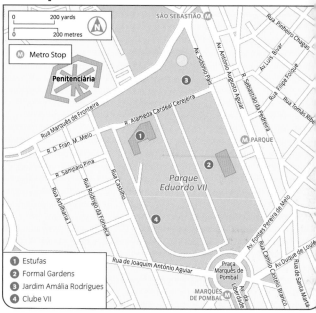

- ❶ Estufas
- ❷ Formal Gardens
- ❸ Jardim Amália Rodrigues
- ❹ Clube VII

F**rom the foot of the Avenida da Liberdade you can see the formal layout** of Parque Eduardo VII, the city center's foremost stretch of greenery, crisscrossed by paths and carefully trimmed hedges. On Sundays it seems that half the city is here strolling, playing sport, meeting friends, taking their kids to the play areas, picnicking, or feeding ducks on the lake. START: **Metro: Parque, Pombal. Bus: 1, 2, 11, 12, 18, 22, 23, 27, 31, 36, 42, 44, 45, 48, 51, 83, 90, 91, 113, 115, 718, 742, 746.**

Feed the ducks at the lake.

The formal gardens at Parque Eduardo VII.

① ★ Estufas. The park takes on an exotic look in its *estufas* (greenhouses) of tropical plants, well worth the small fee to see inside. The Estufa Fria are unheated greenhouses with flora from around the world. Paths lead you past waterfalls, ponds and grottos, built from a former quarry. In the heated Estufa Quente (hothouse), you'll find plants such as coffee and mango, and the tiny Estufa Doce (sweet) houses cacti such as golden barrel and aloe vera. ☎ 21-388-2278. *Admission 1.53€; 0.77€ youth card holders, seniors; free under 12. Open Apr–Sep 9am–5.30pm; Oct–Mar 9am–4.30pm.*

② Formal Gardens. The park's most eye-catching features (and the main area of the park) are the beds, hedges and pathways of the formal gardens, visible from far away. Stroll along the pathways and stop for ice cream, coffee or lunch at the lakeside Botequim do Rei.

③ ★ Jardim Amália Rodrigues. This small garden is dedicated to Amália Rodrigues, Lisbon's much-feted fado *queen* (p 38). There's a café-bar looking across a lake, a bronze of a mother and child by Colombian sculptor Carlos Botero called *Maternidade*, and the Michelin-starred restaurant, Eleven (p 108). *Alameda Cardeal Cerejeira, Alto do Parque. Open 24 hours a day. Bus: 718, 742, 746, 203.*

④ Clube VII. If you want a workout in the gym, a swim in the indoor pool, or a game of tennis, this is a particularly well set-up sports facility in the city center. Guests of Le Meridien Park Atlantic Lisbon (see p 144), can take advantage of the hotel's membership here. *Parque Eduardo VII.* ☎ 808-277-288; www.clubevii.com. *Open Tues–Fri 7am–10.30pm; Sat 7am–10.30pm; Sat 9am–9pm; Sun & public holidays 10am–6pm.*

Maternidade sculpture by Carlos Botero

City Center Gardens

| | 0 | 200 yards |
| | 0 | 200 metres |

M Metro Stop

R. Alameda Cardeal Cerejeira
Av. Sidónio Pais
R. Sebastião da Pedreira
Av. António Augusto Aguiar

Estufa Fria

PARQUE Ⓜ

Rua Marquês de Fronteira
R. D. Fran. M. Melo
R. Sampaio Pina
Rua Castilho
Rua Rodrigo da Fonseca
Rua Artilharia 1
Av. Cons. Fernando de Sousa

Parque Eduardo VII

Ⓢ

Av. Fontes Pereira de Melo

Rua de Joaquim António Aguiar

Praça Marquês de Pombal

MARQUÊS DE POMBAL Ⓜ

Rua Carmo Castelo Branco
Rua Rodrigues Sampaio
Av. da Liberdade

Rua das Amoreiras
Rua Silva Carvalho
Tv. Fab. das Sedas
Rua S. Filipe Nery
Ⓢ
Rua Braancamp
Rua Duque de Palmela
Rua Mouzinho da Silveira
Rua Rosa Araújo
Rua Barata Salgueiro

Rua Dom João V
Rua do Sol do Rato
Rua da Arrábida
Largo do Rato
RATO Ⓜ
Rua Alexandre Herculano
Rua Castilho
Rua da Escola Politécnica

São Mamede †

Rua Nova de S. Mamede
Rua do Salitre
AVENIDA Ⓜ

Rua de São Bento
Rua do Arco de S. Mamede

Jardim Botánico

Ⓢ

Tv. do Salitre
Praça da Alegria

Av. Álvares Cabral
Tv. Sta. Quitéria
Rua de S. Bernardo
Ⓢ
Rua da Imprensa Nacional
Rua Prazeres
Cç. Engº Miguel Pais
R. dpr Monte Olivete
Tv. do Monte do Carmo
Tv. Monte
R. Cecílio de Sousa
R. da Alegria
CC da Patriarcal
Tv. do Rosário
Rua das Taip

Rua de Santo Amaro

Rua Nova Piedade
Rua de S. Marçal
R. das Adelas
R. do Jasmim
R. da Palmeira Real
R. D. Pedro V
Ⓢ

R. Conde de Soure
R. Luísa Todi
Tv. de S. Pedro
Tv. R. dos
R. Nova do Loureiro
Rua Vinha
R. de Cabra
Tv. da Boa Hora
Tv. da Água de Flor
R. do Teixeira
R. dos Mouros

Rua de São Bento
Rua da Cruz Polais
Rua da Quintinha
Rua Eduardo Coelho
Tv. da Horta
Rua Academia Ciências
Rua do Século
Tv. dos Inglesinhos
Tv. da Queimada

Largo de Jesus

BAIRRO ALTO

① Jardim da Estrela
② Jardim do Principe Real
③ Jardim das Amoreiras
④ Jardim Botanico
⑤ Parque Eduardo VII
⑥ Jardim da Fundação Calouste Gulbenkian

Despite its density, Lisbon's not claustrophobia-inducing, thanks to its spacious squares and peaceful gardens, overflowing with greenery and water features. And here and there you encounter many spectacular miradouros (viewing points) that make the most of the city's dramatic changes in height. START: **Jardim da Estrela. Tram: 25, 28. Bus: 9, 720, 738, 773.**

1 ★ kids **Jardim da Estrela.** Spacious and leafy, this is a great park to take the smaller kids for a picnic, especially after walking those tough cobbled hills; they may find new verve when they see the toddlers' playpark. *Praça da Estrela.* ☎ *21-397-4818. Admission free. Open daily 7am–12am. Tram: 25, 28. Bus: 9, 720.*

2 ★ kids **Jardim do Príncipe Real.** It's surprising what you can fit into such a small space. Even though there's a café at either end, a kids' play area and an underground water museum (a former waterworks revealing an eerily drippy, subterranean world), it has ample green spaces for a picnic. *Praça do Príncipe Real. Admission free. Water Museum Admission 2.50€; students, Lisboa Card, seniors 2.50€; under 12 free. Open Tues–Sat 10am–6pm. Park open 24 hours a day. Bus: 58, 790.*

3 ★★ **Jardim das Amoreiras.** This small park is one that I regularly return to when visiting Lisbon, which

The tranquil Jardim Botanico.

stands out because of the short section of aqueduct that passes along one side with tiled panels on its outer walls (p 77). The *amoreiras*, or mulberry trees, once here to supply a nearby silk factory, have long gone, but it's still a pleasantly shady retreat from the summer heat. *Praça das Amoreiras. Open 24 hours a day. Metro: Rato. Bus: 58, 74.*

4 **Jardim Botanico.** This is a tranquil and shaded oasis with winding paths, small lakes, and benches below towering palms. There's various species of them along with orchids and other tropical plants, and the butterfly house is a spectacular corner of color. *Rua da Escola Politécnica, 58.* ☎ *21-392-1800; www.jb. ul.pt. Admission 1.50€; 0.75€ seniors, students, youth card holders; free under 6. Open Apr–Oct Mon–Fri 9am–8pm; Sat & Sun 10am–8pm; Nov–Mar Mon–Fri 9am–6pm; Sat & Sun 10am–6pm. Bus: 58 (stops outside entrance), 92, 711, 790. Metro: Rato.*

5 ★★ **Parque Eduardo VII.** See p 92.

6 ★★ **Jardim da Fundação Calouste Gulbenkian.** These grounds have been carefully designed with pathways, various species of tropical and native plants, plus some striking sculptures. I find it the ideal tonic to being "museumed" out. *Avenida de Berna, 45A.* ☎ *21-782-3000. Admission 4€, 20% discount Lisboa Card; 50% discount seniors/students; free under 12. Open Tue–Sun 10am–5.45pm. Metro: São Sebastião/Praça de Espanha. Bus: 16, 26, 31, 46, 56.*

Parque Florestal de **Monsanto & Belém**

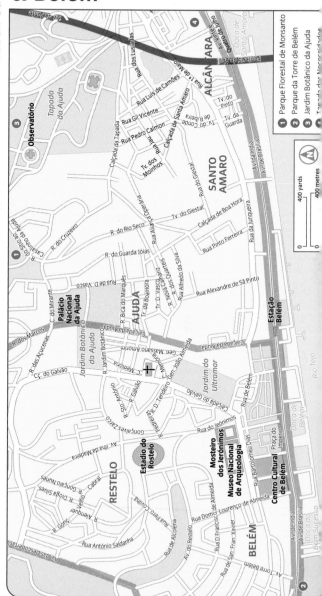

1 Parque Florestal de Monsanto
2 Parque da Torre de Belém
3 Jardim Botânico da Ajuda
4 Tapada das Necessidades

ALCÂNTARA

Observatório
Tapada da Ajuda

SANTO AMARO

AJUDA

Palácio Nacional da Ajuda

Jardim Botânico da Ajuda

Jardim do Ultramar

Estação Belém

RESTELO

Estádio do Restelo

Mosteiro dos Jerónimos

Museo Nacional de Arqueologia

Centro Cultural de Belém

Praça do Império

BELÉM

Rio Tejo

Doca de Belém

0   400 yards
0   400 metres

Rua dos Lusíadas
Rua Luís de Camões
Rua Gil Vicente
Rua Pedro Calmon
Calçada de Santa Amaro
Calçada da Tapada
Tv. dos Moinhos
Tv. do Pinto
Tv. da Guarda
Rua do Giestal
Tv. do Giestal
Calçada de Boa Hora
Rua da Junqueira
Rua Pinto Ferreira
R. do Cruzeiro
R. do Rio Seco
R. do Guarda Jóias
Rua Aliança Operária
Rua dos Quartéis
Rua Alfredo da Silva
Rua Alexandre de Sá Pinto
C. do Mirante
R. dos Marcos
R. das Açucenas
Cç. do Galvão
R. de D. Vasco
R. da Boa Hora
R. Bica do Marquês
Tr. D. Vasco
R. Nova Calhariz
Tr. da Memória
C. Memória
R. Jardim Botânico
Gen. Massano Amorim
Calçada da Ajuda
Gen. João Almeida
Calçada do Galvão
Rua de Belém
R. São António
R. Galvão
R. Pardelhas
R. D. Tenderio
Gonçalves Zarco
Rua do Jerónimos
Av. Ilha da Madeira
Av. do Restelo
R. Gonç. Velho
R. Diogo Silves
R. Gonçalo Nunes
R. Alenquer
R. de Alcolena
Rua Pero Covilhã
Rua D. Francisco de Almeida
Rua Domo Lourenço de Almeida
Rua Bartolomeu Dias
Rua António Saldanha
Av. de San. Fran. Xavier
Av. Torre Belém
Av. de Brasília
Av. da Índia
Doca do Bem Sucesso
Av. das Descobertas
Ponte 25 de Abril
Quinta do Jardim
Doca de Santo Amaro
Av. da Ponte
Rua 1.º de Maio
Tv. do Conde de R. Ibeira
R. do Sítio ao Casalinho da Ajuda
Cabral

What I love about west Lisbon is that it has retained its sense of space with green spaces from the vast Parque Florestal de Monsanto to Torre de Belém's shady waterfront park. Stop for a picnic in the shade, take in the floral scents of tropical gardens or opt for something sporty.

① kids Parque Florestal de Monsanto. There's no problem finding something to keep kids active at these three popular play-parks. Pedreira da Serafina is a wooded area with sheer rock faces, great for walks and climbing, while Mata de São Domingos de Benfica is an adventure park with a climbing wall. Or you can bike or roller-blade along the network of paths and small roads, play tennis, picnic or have lunch at a restaurant. In the north part of the park is the Palácio dos Marqueses da Fronteira, with the Jardim Zoologico de Lisboa just beyond it (p 33). *Information Estrada do Barcal, Monte das Perdizes.* ☎ *21-817-0200. Bus: 29 (south),*

Decorative tile at the Palacio dos Marqueses da fronteira

24 (southeast), 11, 23 (east), 70 (north), 24, 29 (west).

② Parque da Torre de Belém. By the Belém Tower (p 14), this compact park suits me just fine; it's lush with plenty of shade, a clear tower and river view and perfect for re-energizing. Just the spot for a picnic, though kids might make a beeline for the adjacent Haagen-Dazs store for an ice cream. *Avenida de Brasília. Train: Belém. Tram: 15. Bus: 27, 28, 29, 43, 49, 51, 112.*

③ Jardim Botânico d'Ajuda. Breathe in the scents of flora, trees and flowers from former Portuguese colonies in Portugal's first botanic garden. Planted in 1768, it has

There are relaxing gardens beside the Torre de Belém.

Keen gardeners will enjoy a visit to Jardim da Ajuda.

retained its Renaissance layout with pathways, lakes, shaped hedges and beds, plus the later addition of a baroque fountain and steps. A seasonal festival of color, this is definitely one for the gardeners. *Calçada da Ajuda s/n.* ☎ *21-362-2503. Admission 2€; 1€ students, seniors; free under 7 & Sun. Open Apr daily 9am–7pm; May–Sep daily 9am–8pm; Oct–Mar daily 9am–6pm. Tram: 18. Bus: 14, 27, 29, 32.*

④ ★ **Tapada das Necessidades** Within walking distance of Lisbon's renovated docklands, these former royal gardens make a lush inner-city escape, attached to a 17th-century palace (now the Ministry for Foreign Affairs). Various Portuguese kings had a hand in shaping the gardens. Wander amongst its lakes, palm trees, curious round greenhouse, statues, and cacti collection. *Largo das Necessidades.* ☎ *21-446-3700. Admission free. Open Apr–Oct daily 10am–9.30pm; Nov–Mar daily 10am–6.30pm. Bus: 713, 720.* ●

Getting Around Parque Florestal de Monsanto

Monsanto Park is a vast area and somewhat off-putting to the casual foot who arrives on foot. Pedestrians are most likely to visit the peripheries of the park via the Palacio dos Marqueses da Fronteira (bus 70) on the north side of the park or the Jardim Botânico da Ajuda (bus 14, 73) in the south. For exploring the park further, or for those that want to stay at the campsite here (see p 144), a car or at least a bicycle is a must. This isn't the kind of park for gentle afternoon strolls on your own; as sometimes it can feel quite remote (except for the major road passing through it), so you should take at least one other person with you. If in doubt, seek advice from the Information Centre here or the Lisbon Welcome Centre in the city centre.

Alfama Dining

Bico do Sapato **1**
Casa do Leão **2**
Dragão do Alfama **3**
Jardim do Marisco **4**
Restaurante Faz Figura **5**

ⓘ Information
Ⓜ Metro Stop
Ⓟ Car Park

Parque das Nações Dining

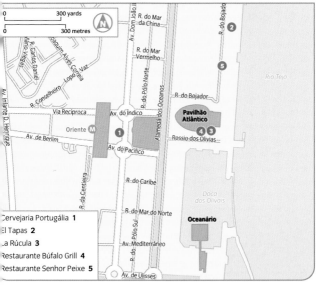

Cervejaria Portugália **1**
El Tapas **2**
La Rúcula **3**
Restaurante Búfalo Grill **4**
Restaurante Senhor Peixe **5**

The Best Dining

City Center Dining

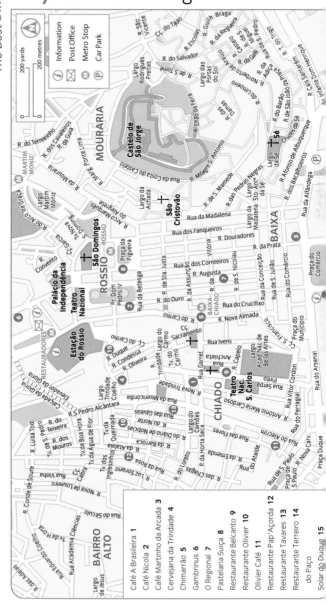

Information
Post Office
Metro Stop
Car Park

200 yards
200 metres

Café A Brasileira 1
Café Nicola 2
Café Martinho da Arcada 3
Cervejaria da Trindade 4
Chimarrão 5
Gambrinus 6
O Regional 7
Pastelaria Suíça 8
Restaurante Belcanto 9
Restaurante Olivier 10
Olivier Café 11
Restaurante Pap'Açorda 12
Restaurante Tavares 13
Restaurante Terreiro do Paço 14
Solar do Duque 15

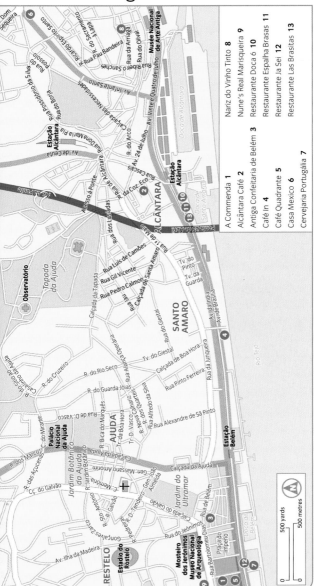

North of City Center Dining

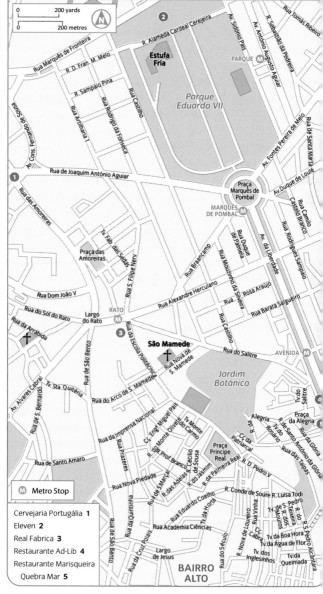

M Metro Stop

Cervejaria Portugália **1**

Eleven **2**

Real Fabrica **3**

Restaurante Ad-Lib **4**

Restaurante Marisqueira
Quebra Mar **5**

Lisbon Dining **A to Z**

★★ A Commenda BELEM
MEDITERRANEAN Dine on dishes
such as fresh tuna with olive dress-
ing or Iberian pork with regional
stuffing. As well as occasional
themed musical evenings and Sunday buffets, there's a large terrace
overlooking the river. *Centro Cultural
de Belém, Praça do Imperio.*
☎ *21-361-2610. Entrees 15€–22€;
set menu 33€. AE, MC, V. Lunch &
dinner daily, lunch only Sun. Tram:
15. Map p 103.*

★★ Alcântara Café ALCANTARA
MODERN PORTUGUESE A mixture
of modern industrial décor, gilt-
edged mirrors and a large Helenistic
statue of Vitória de Samutrácia, this
warehouse restaurant aims to be a
"modern classic", with inventive
Portuguese cuisine. Reservations
advised. *Rua Maria Luisa Holstein
15.* ☎ *21-363-7176. Entrees
25€–35€. AE, MC, V. Dinner daily.
Tram: 12. Map p 103.*

**★★★ Antiga Confeitaria de
Belém** BELEM *CAFÉ* Dating back
to 1837 and firmly on the tourist
trail, this historic café won't disap-
point. Either go local and stand at
the crowded front counter to order
um café (small black coffee) and a
pastel, their famed custard tart. Or

go into the warren of tile-covered
back rooms for waiter service. *Rua
de Belém, 84-92.* ☎ *21-363-7423.
Coffee/tea & pastel 1€–3€. Daily.
Tram: 15. Map p 103.*

★ Café Quadrante BELEM *INTER-
NATIONAL* The Belém Cultural
Center's self-service restaurant is a
good option for lunches/early din-
ners such as quiche and salad, or
lasagne. *Avenida Brasília, Ed. Apoio
á Naútico.* ☎ *21-362-0865. Centro
Cultural de Belém, Praça do Imperio.*
☎ *21-362-9256. Entrees 5€–8€. AE,
MC, V. Lunch & dinner daily. Tram: 15.
Map p 103.*

★★★ Bica do Sapato ALFAMA
PORTUGUESE Whether you
choose the café for seafood rice and
grilled pork, or the pricier restaurant
for beef tornedo, suckling pig and
trilogy of *bacalhau* (cod), this
renowned restaurant is about
quality, contemporary style, and
river views. There's also a good
quality sushi bar. *Avenida Dom
Henrique, Arm. B, Cais da Pedra.*
☎ *21-881-320. Entrees 14€–38€.
AE, MC, V. Restaurant lunch & dinner
Tues–Sat, dinner only Mon; Cafeteria
lunch & dinner, snacks & dinner only
Mon; sushi bar dinner Mon–Sat.
Bus: 6, 12, 34. Map p 101.*

Antiga Confeitaria de Belém.

★★ Café A Brasileira CHIADO

PORTUGUESE/CAFÉ Renowned for the bronze statue of modernist poet Fernando Pessoa outside, this historic café doesn't have the politest waiters, but using a few words of Portuguese might help. It has retained interior dark-wood décor and chandeliers, and if you want more than a cake or toasted sandwich, head downstairs for a reasonable Portuguese lunch. *Rua Garrett, 120. ☎ 21-346-9541. Coffee & cake 2€–4€; Entrees 7€–9€. AE, MC, V. Daily; downstairs lunch only. Closed Aug. Tram: 15. Map p 102.*

★ Café Nicola BAIXA *CAFÉ*

Another historic café once frequented by Lisbon intellectuals, its modernist façade faces Rossio Square. Stand at the counter for a quick coffee. If you sit down you'll pay double or more. *Praça Dom Pedro IV. ☎ 21-346 0579. Coffee & cake 2€–4€, Mon–Sat. Closed Sun. Metro: Rossio. Tram: 15. Map p 102.*

★★ Café In BELEM *PORTUGUESE/ INTERNATIONAL* This specializes in charcoal-grilled fish and fresh seafood. I find its position and terrace overlooking the river really special. *Avenida Brasília, Pavilhão Nascente. ☎ 21-362-6248. Entrees 15€–25€. AE, MC, V. Lunch & dinner daily. Tram: 15. Map p 103.*

★★ Café Martinho da Arcada

BAIXA *PORTUGUESE/CAFÉ* Lisbon's oldest café, first founded in 1778, it was another haunt of the poet Fernando Pessoa and you'll see a table still laid for him in the restaurant. Dine on *bacalhau* (cod) or tender baked goat or just stop for a coffee in the café, an attractive combination of wooden bar and typical tiles. *Praça do Comércio, 3. ☎ 21-886-6213. Coffee & cake 1.50€–3€. Entrees 12€–18€. AE, DC, MC, V. Lunch & dinne, Mon–Sat. Tram: 15, 25, 28. Metro: Baixa-Chaido. Map p 102.*

★★★ Casa do Leão ALFAMA

PORTUGUESE In the grounds of the castle, with vaulted ceilings, tiled walls and bar, this upmarket Portuguese venue is for a special night out. Expect fine Portuguese cuisine from skewers of fresh fish to tender steaks and local cheeses. Book ahead. *Castelo de São Jorge. ☎ 21-888-0154. Entrees 18€–30€. AE, MC, V. Lunch & dinner daily. Tram: 28. Bus: 37. Map p 101.*

Café Martinho da Arcada.

Cervejaria da Trindade.

★★ **Casa México** ALCANTARA
MEXICAN Bright, fun and funky
décor combines with the usual Mexican enchiladas and nachos plus a
tasty surprise starter of battered pork
and strawberry sauce dip. The jugs of
sangria are well prepared. *Avenida
Dom Carlos I.* ☎ 21-397-4790.
*Entrees 8€–14€. AE, MC, V. Lunch
Mon–Fri, dinner Sat & Sun. Tram: 12,
15. Map p 103.*

★★ **Cervejaria da Trindade**
BAIRRO ALTO *PORTUGUESE* Covered in Portuguese tiles, this is a
relaxed and comfortable beer hall
and restaurant housed in a former
monastery refectory. It offers a
range of beers and I've enjoyed crab
here served on a wooden board
with a hammer. *Rua Nova da
Trindade.* ☎ 21-342-3506. *Entrees
8€–15€. AE, DC, MC, V. Lunch &
dinner daily. Closed public holidays.
Elevador da Gloria. Metro: Restauradores. Map p 102.*

★ kids **Cervejaria Portugália**
BELEM *PORTUGUESE* This reliable
chain of restaurants (some in shopping centers) serves affordable Portuguese cuisine, including steaks in
gravy topped with ham and egg, a
range of prawn dishes and a kids'
menu. *Avenida Brasilia, Ed. Espelho
de Agua.* ☎ 21-303-2700. *Entrees
8€–13€. AE, MC, V. Lunch & dinner
daily. Tram: 15. Map p 101.*

Amoreiras Shopping. ☎ 21-384-
4796. *Entrees 8€–13€. AE, MC, V.
Lunch & dinner daily. Metro: Rato.*
Centro Comercial Vasco da Gama.
☎ 21-011-482. *Entrees 8€–13€.
AE, MC, V. Lunch & dinner daily.
Metro: Oriente.*

★ kids **Chimarrão** CHIADO *BRAZIL-
IAN* A popular shopping center
restaurant, this is a Brazilian-style
rodizio (grill) with various all-you-
can-eat options. Pile your plate high
with salad, chips, rice and stacks of
meat, then order a drink at the table.
Some offers also include a drink and
dessert. *Rua do Carmo, Armazens do*

*Enjoy a platter of oysters in Cervejaria da
Trindade.*

Chiado. ☎ 21-347-9444. All you can eat menu 6€–23€. AE, MC, V. Lunch & dinner daily. Metro: Baixa-Chiado. Map p 102.

Alameda dos Oceanos, Parque das Nações. ☎ 21-895-2222. All you can eat menu 6€–23€. AE, MC, V. Lunch & dinner daily. Metro: Oriente.

Amoreiras Shopping. ☎ 21-386-2363. All you can eat menu 6€–12€. AE, MC, V. Lunch & dinner daily. Metro: Rato.

★ **Dragão do Alfama** ALFAMA PORTUGUESE   A small eaterie with typical blue and white tiles and photos of famous *fado* singers on the walls, with live *fado* on Thursday, Friday and Saturday evenings. The menu includes grilled squid and prawns and oven-baked *bacalhau*. *Rua Guillerme Braga, 8.* ☎ *21-886-777. Entrees 8€–12€. AE, MC, V. Dinner Mon–Sat. Tram: 28. Map p 101.*

★★★ **Eleven** AVENIDA/PARQUE MODERN PORTUGUESE   Lisbon's only Michelin-starred restaurant at the time of writing, it's tastefully styled with contemporary art complementing huge views across the city. Choose from the lunchtime Menu Express or a five-course tasting menu. *Rua Marquês de Fronteira, Jardim Amália Rodrígues.* ☎ *21-386-2211. Lunch express*

menu 39€; tasting menu 79€. AE, DC, MC, V. Lunch & dinner Tues–Sat. Closed public holidays. Metro: Parque. Map p 104.

★ **El Tapas** PARQUE NACOES SPANISH   An airy, warehouse-style building with bullfighting images and Spanish flags. Pick and mix a selection of tapas such as stuffed peppers, meatballs, garlic prawns and spicy potatoes, or opt for a full portion of paella. *Rua do Bojador, 99-101.* ☎ *21-896-900. Tapas 4.50€–8€. AE, DC, MC, V. Lunch & dinner daily. Metro: Oriente. Map p 101.*

★★ **Gambrinus** BAIXA PORTUGUESE/FISH   One of the city's most acclaimed restaurants, with a history dating back decades and a clientele that includes politicians and celebrities. It doesn't come cheap so book ahead and plan on a big night out. *Rua das Portas de S Antão, 23.* ☎ *21-342-1466. Entrees 25€–45€. AE, DC, MC, V. Lunch & dinner daily. Metro: Rossio, Restauradorses. Map p 102.*

★★ **Jardim do Marisco** ALFAMA PORTUGUESE/FISH   In a large warehouse on the waterfront, and a good choice for a varied menu of fresh fish, as well as regional meat dishes. Try Mozambique-style prawns

The Michelin-starred Eleven has fantastic views across the city.

El Tapas.

or Alentejo-style pork. *Jardim do Tabaco, Avenida Dom Henrique.* ☎ 21-882-4240. *Entrees 10€–25€; AE, DC, MC, V. Lunch & dinner Tues–Sat; dinner only Mon. Closed Aug. Bus: 9, 28, 35. Map p 101.*

★★ **La Rúcula** PARQUE NACOES *ITALIAN* This modern Italian restaurant has views of the river, cable car and Pavilhão Atlântico. Choose from a selection of pizzas, pasta and steaks, followed by sweet Italian desserts such as tiramisu. *Rossio dos Olivais.* ☎ 21-892-2747. *Entrees 10€–15€; AE, DC, MC, V. Lunch & dinner daily. Metro: Oriente. Map p 101.*

★★★ **Nariz do Vinho Tinto** ALCANTARA *PORTUGUESE* If, as the name suggests, you have a good nose for red wine, then you'll like the wine list. The restaurant and the menu are traditional, and popular with families: try *prusunto* (cured ham), Portuguese cheeses, whitebait from Horta (Azores) or baked kid. *Rua do Conde.* ☎ 21-395-035. *Entrees 16€–25€. AE, MC, V. Lunch & dinner Tues–Fri; dinner only Sat. Tram: 15, 2.5 Map p 103.*

★★★ **Nune's Real Marisqueira** BELEM *PORTUGUESE/FISH* One of the best-known fish restaurants in the city, this relaxed place serves everything from mussels to lobster and oysters, grouper, salmon and turbot. There's meat too, mostly steaks and skewers, but fish is definitely the order of the day. *Rua Bartolomeu Dias.* ☎ 21-301-9899. *Entrees 15€–25€. AE, MC, V. Lunch & dinner Mon–Sun. Closed Wed. Tram: 15. Map p 103.*

★ **O Regional** BAIXA *PORTUGUESE* Right in the heart of the Baixa, this unassuming restaurant is not on the tourist trail. Authentic Portuguese cuisine such as house-style *bacalhau* with egg, or *churrasco a cafria* (spit-roast meat), with old-fashioned homemade desserts like *arroz doce* (rice pudding). *Rua dos Sapateiros.* ☎ 21-342-1027. *Entrees 8€–12€. AE, DC, MC, V. Lunch & dinner daily. Metro: Baixa-Chiado. Map p 102.*

★★ **Pastelaria Suiça** BAIXA *PORTUGUESE/CAFÉ* This huge and historic café straddles both Rossio and Figueira squares, so you can sit in either one or in the shiny interior, indoor seating. There's a wide range of sinful-looking cakes, many with egg, pastry and dustings of icing sugar. *Praça Dom Pedro IV.* ☎ 21-321-4090. *Coffee & cake 1.50€–4€. AE, MC, V. Daily. Metro: Rossio. Tram: 15. Map p 102.*

★★★ **Restaurante Ad-Lib** AVENIDA *MODERN MEDITERRANEAN* A stylish hotel restaurant with sleek, black tables, autumnal gold and orange décor and original works of art. The food lives up to the setting: truffle-infused soup, pork stuffed with spinach and pine nuts, and lobster ravioli. *Hotel Sofitel Lisboa, Avenida da Liberdade, 127.* ☎ 21-322-8350. *Entrees 18€–30€. AE, DC,*

MC, V. Lunch & dinner daily. Metro: Avenida. Map p 104.

★★★ Restaurante Belcanto

CHIADO *PORTUGUESE/INTERNATIONAL* With a long-standing reputation for quality Portuguese cuisine this is popular for business lunches. Classic dishes get the house treatment, from various baked and grilled fish dishes to roast beef and stroganoff. *Largo de São Carlos.* ☎ *21-342-0607. Entrees 12€–19€. AE, DC, MC, V. Lunch & dinner daily. Metro: Baixa-Chiado. Map p 102.*

★★ Restaurante Búfalo Grill

PARQUE NACOES *BRAZILIAN* My favorite Brazilian *rodizio* (grill) in Lisbon, you'll need plenty of space for the all-you-can-eat deal. This includes a cold buffet, followed by Brazilian black beans, fried banana, rice and liberal slices of meat from steaming skewers. *Rossio dos Olivais, Parque das Nações.* ☎ *21-892-2740. Buffet menu 15€–25€. AE, DC, MC, V. Lunch & dinner daily. Metro: Oriente. Map p 101.*

★★ Restaurante Doca 6

ALCANTARA *MEDITERRANEAN* A few years ago this was *the* place to lunch in the docks. It still merits a visit for its views from both inside and outdoors on the terrace. Dishes include fish skewers, roast duck, and the house beef with a mustard sauce. *Doca de Santo Amaro.* ☎ *21-395-7905. Entrees 10€–18€. AE, DC, MC, V. Lunch & dinner. Closed Mon. Tram: 15. Map p 103.*

★★ Restaurante Faz Figura

ALFAMA *MODERN PORTUGUESE* Aims to be modern Portuguese but has a fairly traditional menu, including oven-cooked kid and stuffed squid. The views over the river give plenty to look at, and there's a good selection of regional wines. *Rua do Paraíso, 15B.* ☎ *21-886-8981. Entrees 15€–20€. AE, MC, V. Lunch & dinner. Tram: 28. Map p 101.*

★ Restaurante Ja Sei

BELEM *PORTUGUESE* A privileged position looking straight out at the Discoveries Monument by the river. Open for

Stylish hotel restaurant Ad-Lib.

Restaurante Bufalo Grill

lunch only, they serve *cataplana* (stew in a copper dish), *bacalhau* and veal escalopes. *Avenida Brasília, 202.* ☎ *21-301-5969. Entrees 12€– 15€. AE, MC, V. Lunch only. Tram: 15. Map p 103.*

★★ Restaurante Las Brasitas
ALCANTARA *PORTUGUESE* This is one for the meat lovers with Argentinean-inspired steaks—not quite as large as the Latin American version. *Doca de Santo Amaro, Arm. 16.* ☎ *21-396-0647. Entrees 15€– 20€. AE, MC, V. Lunch & dinner. Tram: 15. Map p 103.*

★★ Restaurante Marisquiera Quebra Mar
AVENIDA *PORTUGUESE/FISH* Either come here early or book ahead for this popular fish restaurant. You'll see displays of fish in the window and the menu is no less impressive with everything from octopus salad and mixed fish grill to *bacalhau minhota* (salted cod with garlic, cabbage and potatoes, a traditional Christmas dish). *Avenida da Liberdade, 77.* ☎ *21-346-4855. Entrees 15€–20€. AE, DC, MC, V. Lunch & dinner. Metro: Avenida. Map p 104.*

★★ Restaurante Olivier
CHIADO *MODERN FRENCH/PORTUGUESE* Trendy place in Chiado with innovative dishes such as crab guacamole, carpaccio of bullock and scallops with *beurre blanc provencal* sauce. Also pride themselves on the wine but be careful as some bottles top the 1000€ mark. *Rua do Alecrim, 23.* ☎ *21-343-1405. Tasting menu 36€. AE, DC, MC, V. Dinner only. Closed Sun. Tram: 28, Elevador da Glória. Metro: Rossio. Map p 102. Rua do Alecrim, 23.* ☎ *21-342-2916. Tram: 28. Metro: Baixa-Chiado.*

★★★ Restaurante Pap'Açorda
CHIADO *PORTUGUESE* Renowned as one of Lisbon's top restaurants, you'll need to dig deep to dine here. Its menu is traditional but exquisite, including dishes with lobster and prawns, grouper, ribs and kid. *Rua da Atalaia.* ☎ *21-346-4. Entrees 45€–55€. AE, DC, MC, V. Lunch & dinner. Closed Sun & Mon. Metro: Baixa-Chiado Map p 102.*

Restaurante Olivier.

★★ Restaurante Senhor Peixe

PARQUE NACOES *PORTUGUESE/FISH* Smaller than many of the restaurants along this "strip", the fish certainly makes it a popular choice with lobster rice and fish of the day. *Rua da Pimenta.* ☎ *21-895-5892. Entrees 9€–13€. AE, DC, MC, V. Lunch & dinner. Closed Sun & Mon. Metro: Oriente. Map p 101.*

★★★ Restaurante Tavares

BAIRRO ALTO *INTERNATIONAL* Lisbon's oldest restaurant and renowned for its popularity with Portuguese writers such as Eça de Queiros. It doesn't come cheap, but it always employs top chefs. You're greeted by a uniformed doorman and dine in palatial room with glass chandeliers. *Rua da Miseracordia.* ☎ *21-342-1112. Entrees 45€–60€. Tasting menu 65€. AE, DC, MC, V. Dinner. Tram: 28. Map p 102.*

★★★ Restaurante Terreiro do Paço

BAIXA *MODERN PORTUGUESE* Regional Portuguese cuisine with a contemporary twist (sardines in mousse or braised tuna from the Azores). Sleek and modern inside, during warm weather you can dine outside. *Praça do Comércio.* ☎ *21-031-2850. Entrees 18€–25€. AE, MC, V. Lunch & dinner Mon–Fri. Dinner only Sat. Tram: 15, 25. Map p 102.*

★★ Solar do Duque

BAIRRO ALTO *PORTUGUESE* Full of character with hand-painted murals on its façade and rustic interior stone walls. During warm weather, diners spill onto the street outside. *Rua do Duque, 67-69.* ☎ *21-342-6901. Entrees 9€–16€. AE, MC, V. Lunch & dinner. Metro: Rossio. Map p 102.* ●

Nightlife Best Bets

Best **Place** for Ginjinhas
★ Ginjinha do Rossio, *Largo São Domingos* (p 118)

Best **Place** for Port Lovers
★★★ Solar do Vinho do Porto, *Rua de São Pedro de Alcântara, 45* (p 124)

Best **Place** for Fado
★★★ Clube do Fado, *Rua São João da Praça, 94* (p 121)

Best **Bar** for the Over 30s
Belém Terrace, *Centro Cultural de Belém* (p 118)

Best **Club** for the Over 30s
★ Frágil, *Rua da Atalaia, 126* (p 120)

Best **Place** for Cocktails
★★ Janela d'Atalaia, *Rua da Atalaia, 160* (p 120)

Best **Place** for Rock Bands
★★ Paradise Garage, *Rua João de Oliveira Miguéns, 38-48* (p 124)

Best **Gay Bar**
★★★ Gayleria, *Rua de Santa Caterina 28* (p 123)

Best **Gay Disco**
★★ Trumps, *Rua da Imprensa Nacional, 104B* (p 122)

Best **Student Bar**
★ Mezcal, *Travessa da Agua da Flor, 20* (p 119)

Best **Irish Pub**
Hennessey's Irish Pub, *Rua do Cais do Sodré, 32-38* (p 118)

Best **Place** for Dance Music
★★ Lux, *Avenida Dom Henrique* (p 121)

Best **Place** for Jazz
★★ Hot Clube de Portugal, *Rua da Alegría, 39* (p 123)

Best **Karaoke Bar**
★ 100 Norte, *Rua da Pimenta, 107* (p 123)

Best **City Views at Night**
★ Belém Café Bar, *Avenida Brasilia – Pavilhão Poente* (p 118)

Taxis at night.

Alcântara / Belem Nightlife

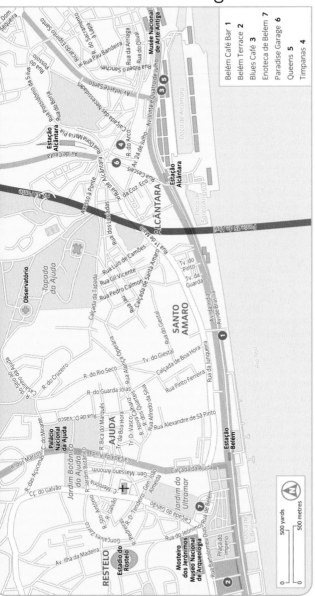

Belém Café Bar **1**
Belém Terrace **2**
Blues Café **3**
Enoteca de Belém **7**
Paradise Garage **6**
Queens **5**
Timpanas **4**

City Center Nightlife

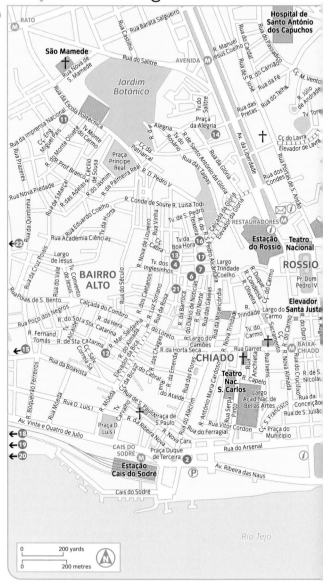

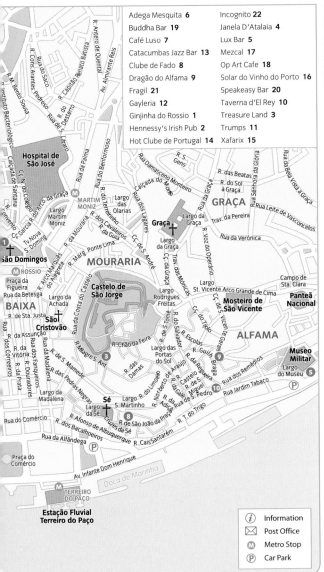

Adega Mesquita **6**
Buddha Bar **19**
Café Luso **7**
Catacumbas Jazz Bar **13**
Clube de Fado **8**
Dragão do Alfama **9**
Fragil **21**
Gayleria **12**
Ginjinha do Rossio **1**
Hennessy's Irish Pub **2**
Hot Clube de Portugal **14**

Incognito **22**
Janela D'Atalaia **4**
Lux Bar **5**
Mezcal **17**
Op Art Cafe **18**
Solar do Vinho do Porto **16**
Speakeasy Bar **20**
Taverna d'El Rey **10**
Treasure Land **3**
Trumps **11**
Xafarix **15**

(i) Information
✉ Post Office
Ⓜ Metro Stop
Ⓟ Car Park

Parque das Nacoes Nightlife

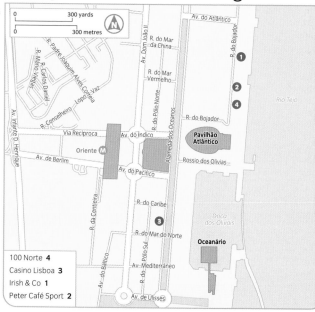

100 Norte **4**
Casino Lisboa **3**
Irish & Co **1**
Peter Café Sport **2**

Lisbon Nightlife A to Z

Bars & Pubs

★★ Belém Café Bar BELEM A large venue with a lounge bar and a terrace (as well as a restaurant with an international menu), and huge windows giving unspoiled views of the 25 de Abril Bridge and the Cristo Rei statue opposite. During the week there's piped ambient music but on Saturday nights it's a livelier scene as DJs play house, hip-hop and R&B. *Avenida Brasília – Pavilhão Poente.* ☎ *21-362-4232. Tram: 15. Map p 115.*

★ Belém Terrace BELEM
Located inside the CCB, this is the place for a quiet drink and gentle background music. At night the view and lights across the Tagus River are impressive. *Centro Cultural de Belém,* ☎ *21-362-0865. Tram: 15. Map p 115.*

★★ Ginjinha do Rossio BAIXA
This hole-in-the wall bar just off Rossio Square is a regular stop-off for people of all ages and walks of life. It only serves *ginjinha*, cherry brandy served in small plastic cups for 1€ a shot. *Largo São Domingos, 8. Metro: Rossio. Map p 117.*

★★ Hennessy's Irish Pub CAIS DO SODRE Popular with both Irish and Brits, this screens major matches and has regular live music, although it's not necessarily Irish. The inside of the bar is decorated like an Irish tailor's with original bric-à-brac. It serves everything from Guinness to Bailey's plus a mixed menu. *Rua do Cais do Sodré, 32-38.* ☎ *21-347-6988. Tram: 15, 25. Metro: Cais do Sodré. Map p 116.*

★★ **Irish & Co** PARQUE DAS NACOES   Part of a chain, it tries hard to be an authentic Irish pub but never quite gets there. However, you can have a good pint of Guinness or Kilkenny and a stout pie. *Rua da Pimenta, 57-61.* ☎ *21-894-0558. Metro: Oriente. Map p 118.*

Irish & Co.

★★ **Mezcal** BAIRRO ALTO   A Mexican-style bar with music and drink to match. During term time, you'll hear every European language being spoken here, as it's a favorite spot with Erasmus exchange students in Lisbon for one or two semesters. By the end of the night, and after too many tequilas, it can get a bit squalid. *Travessa da Agua da Flor, 20.* ☎ *21-343-1863. Tram: 28. Map p 116.*

★★ **Peter Café Sport** PARQUE NACOES PORTUGUESE   The original gin palace and restaurant opened in the Azores in 1918 and remains a favorite stop-off for sailors crossing the Atlantic. Still run by the same family, they opened this venue a few years ago, where you can relax on the terrace with a G&T or two. *Avenida do Borador X. Metro: Oriente. Map p 118.*

Treasure Land ALFAMA   Located just down from the castle, Treasure Land is a small, simple and cozy bar where you can enjoy a couple of beers and a plate of sardines. *Rua Bartolomeu de Gusmão, 11-13.* ☎ *21-886-3960. Tram: 28. Map p 117.*

Casinos

Casino Lisboa PARQUE DAS NACOES   This modern casino in Nations' Park is nearer to the city center than the one in Estoril (p 157). The gambling rooms include black

Try this traditional cherry brandy in Ginjinha do Rossio.

jack and poker, plus there's a lounge bar, live music, restaurants, and glamorous shows. Remember to dress smartly and take some ID. *Alameda dos Oceanos. ☎ 21-466-7700. Metro: Oriente. Map p 118.*

★★ **Casino do Estoril** See p 157.

Cocktail Bars

★ **Janela D'Atalaia** BAIRRO ALTO A trendy *favela chic* (deliberately scruffy mixed with a shot of glamour) bar in the heart of the Bairro Alto, it is hooked on making cocktails, from *mojitos* to *caipirinhas* and jugs of *sangria*. Many local artists exhibit work here; if you see something you want to buy, just ask at the bar. *Rua da Atalaia, 160. ☎ 21-345-6988. Metro: Baixa-Chiado. Tram: 28. Map p 117.*

★★ **Op Art Café** ALCANTARA A café and restaurant by day, Op Art transforms itself into a late-night dance venue. Its funky décor of geometrical designs, long cocktail list, enviable riverside location almost touching 25 de Abril Bridge and guest DJs, means it has no problem attracting hordes of dance music

fans looking for a late night out. *Doca de Santo Amaro. ☎ 21-395-6787. Tram: 15. Map p 116.*

Dance Clubs

★★ **Blues Café** ALCANTARA Popular for its restaurant with a modern international menu, but from 2am its classy club takes over with a mix of jazz, blues and dance sounds. Spread over 4 floors, you can relax with friends in a retro-modern atmosphere with large red lightshades, fringed table lamps, and potted palms. *Rua Cintura Porto, Armazen H. ☎ 21-395-7085. Tram: 15. Map p 115.*

★★ **Buddha Bar** ALCANTARA An exotic club with an oriental theme to the décor. Guest DJs spin deep house and dance music, but you can escape from the dance floor to one of the chill-out areas. *Gare Marítima de Alcântara. ☎ 21-395-0555. Tram: 15. Map p 116.*

★★★ **Frágil** BAIRRO ALTO This is a veteran club and bar popular with 30 and 40 somethings. You can expect to hear a mix of drum 'n' bass, reggae and samba in a down-to-earth atmosphere. It also hosts

Check out the four floors at the Blues Café.

Lux Bar is Lisbon's most famous clubbing venue.

everything from karaoke to bingo. *Rua da Atalaia, 126.* ☎ *21-346-9578. Tram: 28. Map p 116.*

★★ Lux Bar (and Club) APOLONIA   This is Lisbon's most famous club, a legendary dance, drum 'n' bass, hip-hop club that pulls in the punters for top DJs. Turn up late and you face long lines and ridiculous entrance charges that will leave your wallet empty. Inside, it's everything you'd expect from a top club with stylish décor, sofas to lounge on, and even a giant birdcage with dancers. *Avenida Dom Henrique.* ☎ *21-840-4977. Bus: 6, 12, 24. Map p 117.*

Fado

Adega Mesquita BAIRRO ALTO A *fado* house with a long tradition of live performances, this is a popular choice for enjoying traditional Portuguese food as well as the *fado* itself. Music from 8pm. *Rua Diário de Notícias, 107.* ☎ *21-321-9280. Dinner & show 35€–50€. Tram: 28. Map p 117.*

Café Luso BAIRRO ALTO   A veteran *fado* Portuguese restaurant,

dating back to 1927, in the basement of a former palace, with a nightly folkloric dance group in traditional dress, followed by live *fado*. After 1am you can come just to listen to the music. There is also a bar next door where jazz musicians are regularly invited. *Travessa da Queimada, 10.* ☎ *21-342-2281. Dinner & show 40€–45€; drink & show 25€. Metro: Baixa-Chiado. Map p 117.*

★★ Clube de Fado ALFAMA PORTUGUESE   Owned by *fado* guitarist Mario Pachecho and located behind the cathedral, this is a quality venue with performances during dinner and a menu of Portuguese cuisine. It's not cheap but worth it at least once, and Mario usually performs himself. *Rua São João da Praça, 94.* ☎ *21-885-2704. Dinner & show 44€–60€; Tram: 28. Map p 117.*

★★ Dragão do Alfama ALFAMA Located in the heart of the Alfama, this is actually a restaurant with live *fado* music on Thursday, Friday and Saturday. A far cry from the venues aimed at the tourists; Teresa Salgueiro, a singer with Madredeus, was reputedly 'discovered' here.

Catch traditional folk dancing and fado at Café Luso.

Rua Guillerme Braga, 8. 📞 *21-886-777. Entrees 8€–12€. Tram: 28. Map p 117.*

Taverna d'El Rey BAIRRO ALTO This rustic Alfama house was opened by *fadista* Maria Jô Jô four decades ago. Today you can still enjoy her melancholic voice and enjoy a traditional Portuguese menu. *Largo do Chafariz de Dentro, 15.* 📞*21-887-6754/ Dinner & show 25€–50€. Tram: 28. Map p 117.*

Dancers at Trumps.

Timpanas ALCANTARA This *fado* house has been entertaining visitors since 1963. The menu is a mixture of Portuguese and Mediterranean cuisine and there are folkloric and *fado* performances nightly. *Rua Gilberto Rola, 24.* 📞*21-390-6555. Dinner & show 40€–45€; drink & show 30€. Tram: 15. Map p 115.*

Gay & Lesbian Bars/Clubs

Trumps BAIRRO ALTO/RATO Lisbon's trendiest gay venue, Trumps has a café, bars and a dance club spread over 2 floors. The décor is a mixture of metal, glitter and neon lighting downstairs, black floor and trendy chandeliers upstairs. The music is pop/house, plus there are regular shows with everything from flame throwers to drag. *Rua da Imprensa Nacional, 104B.* 📞 *21-397-1059. Metro: Rato. Map p 117.*

★★ **Queens** ALCANTARA Lisbon's largest gay club, Queens is in the renovated Alcântra docks in a huge warehouse, with a bright neon front. It's large, loud and brash with plenty of flashing lights, attracting a mixed crowd for all-night house music. There's also an outdoor terrace and bar, where you can cool off. *Rua de Cintura do Porto, Armazen H.* 📞 *21-395-5870. Tram: 15. Map p 115.*

★★ **Gayleria** WATERFRONT More than a bar, this is the first gay art venue in Lisbon with thematic exhibitions and events. *Rua de Santa Catarina, 28.* ☎ *21-346-1042. Tram: 28. Elevador da Bica. Map p 117.*

Jazz Bars

★★ **Catacumbas Jazz Bar** BAIRRO ALTO On a street renowned for its trendy bars, and a good alternative to the expensive *fado* nights in other parts of the Bairro Alto. You'll find a younger crowd here as well as former students of the Hot Clube de Portugal jazz school performing. *Travesia Agua da Flor, 43.* ☎ *21-346-3969. Tram: 28. Map p 117.*

★★ **Hot Clube de Portugal** AVENIDA Portugal's first 'jazz cave', this club is linked to the jazz school next door. Some of Portugal's best jazz musicians have started out here, so it's a good place to catch a few up-and-coming stars. *Rua da Alegria, 39.* ☎ *21-361-9740. Metro: Avenida. Map p 117.*

★★ **Speakeasy Bar** ALCANTARA This large bar and restaurant has a relaxed feel, with bare brick walls plastered with images of musicians and singers. Although jazz is regularly on the agenda, you can also expect to hear anything from rock to *fado*, so check in advance to make sure it's to your taste. *Cais das Oficinas, Armazen 115.* ☎ *21-390-9166. Tram: 15. Map p 116.*

Karaoke

★ **100 Norte** PARQUE NACOES PORTUGUESE Portuguese restaurant by day, this spacious venue transforms effortlessly into a disco. If you want a sing-song, go here on Tuesday for its karaoke night. *R da Pimenta, 107.* ☎ *21-895-8248. Entrees 12€–16€. AE, MC, V. Lunch & dinner daily, Nov–Mar closed Tues. Metro: Oriente. Map p 118.*

Rock/Alternative Venues

★★ **Incognito Bar** BAIRRO ALTO You'll have to be pretty clued-up to go to this cool underground spot,

Trumps, Lisbon's trendiest gay venue.

The relaxed Speakeasy Bar.

and that's just to find the right door as it's unmarked. Located on two levels, there's post-rock, indie and techno music on different nights. *Rua Poiais de São Bento, 37.* ☎ *21-390-8755. Tram: 28. Map p 116.*

★★ **Paradise Garage** ALCAN-TARA   The foremost venue for live music in Lisbon, with everything from rock concerts to international house DJs and gay nights. *Rua João de Oliveira Miguéns, 38-48.* ☎ *21-324-3400. Tram: 15. Map p 115.*

★★ **Xafariz** ALCANTARA   Originally opened by Portuguese singer Luis Represas, it was taken over a couple of years ago and given a makeover. It turned out to be a good move considering all the new trendy bars in the nearby renovated docks, and Xafariz remains a popular venue for live music from pop to rock. *Avenida Dom Carlos I.* ☎ *21-396-9487. Tram: 15. Map p 117.*

Wine (& Port) Bars

★★★ **Solar do Vinho do Porto** BAIRRO ALTO   This gently sophisticated bar is the perfect place to relax at the end of a day's sightseeing. Sink into a comfortable sofa and try a few port wines, which can range hugely in price. You don't have to spend a fortune to get something palatable though, and you can accompany it with a plate of bread and cheeses. *Rua de São Pedro de Alcântara, 45.* ☎ *21-347-5707. Daily. Metro: Restauradores. Map p 117.*

★★ **Enoteca de Belém** BELEM   Opened in 2007, this is one of Portugal's new breed of wine bars. It's a good place to sample the country's regional wines by the glass or by the carafe, if you already know what you like. *Rua do Marta Pinto, 10/12. Tram: 15. Map p 115.* ●

Arts & Entertainment Best Bets

Best Concert Acoustics
★★★ Fundação Calouste Gulbenkian, *Avenida da Berna (p 129)*

Best Opera House
★★★ Teatro Nacional de São Carlos, *Rua de Serpa Pinto, 9 (p 129)*

Best for Contemporary Performance Arts
★★★ Centro Cultural de Belém, *Praça do Império (p 129)*

Best Ballet Venue
★★ Teatro Camões, *Paseo Neptuno (p 130)*

Best Sporting Event
★★★ SL Benfica, *Avenida Lusiada (p 131)*

Best Theater Performances
★★★ Teatro Nacional de Dona Maria II, *Praça Dom Pedro IV (p 132)*

Best Place for Musicals
★★ Coliseu dos Recreios, *Rua das Portas de Santo Antão (p 129)*

Best Place for Major Concerts
★★★ Pavilhão Atlântico, *Rossio dos Olivais (p 129)*

Best Place for Performance Workshops
★ Chapitô, *Costa do Castelo, 1-7 (p 131)*

Best Fringe Arts Center
★★ Culturgest, *Rua Arco do Cego (p 131)*

Best Moviehouse for a Premier
★★ Cinema Londres, *Avenida da Liberdade, 174 (p 130)*

Best Moviehouse for Blockbusters
★★ El Corte Inglés, *Avenida Antonio Augusto Aguiar (p 131)*

Best Moviehouse for Obscure Films
★ Cinemateca, *Rua Barata Salgueiro, 39 (p 130)*

Teatro Nacional de Dona Maria II.

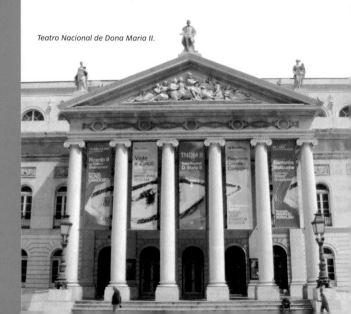

Campo Pequeno Arts & Entertainment

Cinema Londres 2
Culturgest 4
Estádio José de Alvalade 5
Fundação Calouste Gulbenkian 1
UCI - El Corte Inglés 3

Belém Arts & Entertainment

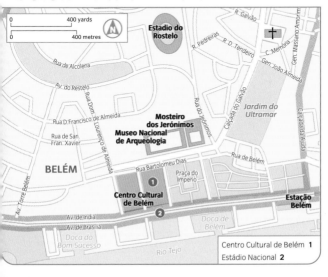

Centro Cultural de Belém 1
Estádio Nacional 2

City Center Arts & Entertainment

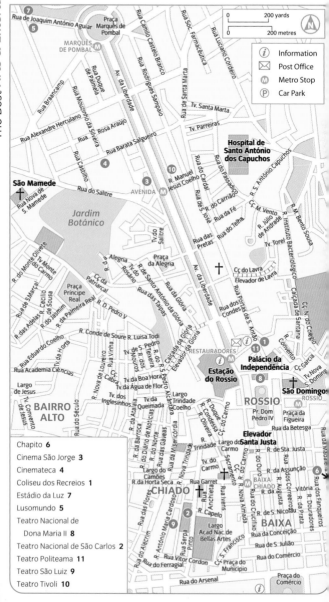

0	200 yards
0	200 metres

- ⓘ Information
- ✉ Post Office
- Ⓜ Metro Stop
- Ⓟ Car Park

Chapito **6**

Cinema São Jorge **3**

Cinemateca **4**

Coliseu dos Recreios **1**

Estádio da Luz **7**

Lusomundo **5**

Teatro Nacional de Dona Maria II **8**

Teatro Nacional de São Carlos **2**

Teatro Politeama **11**

Teatro São Luiz **9**

Teatro Tivoli **10**

Arts & Entertainment **A to Z**

Classical Music & Concert Venues

★★ Centro Cultural de Belém

BELEM   In the past decade the CCB has become the major cultural center for contemporary arts in Lisbon. As well as local and international orchestras and festivals, you can expect classical recitals and performances by a top line-up of jazz and contemporary musicians. In addition, the CCB hosts a full contemporary dance and theater program with some of the most innovative performances from around the world. *Praça do Império.* ☎ *21-361-2400. www.ccb.pt. Tram: 15. Map p 127.*

★★ Coliseu dos Recreios

BAIXA   This historic venue dates back to the late 19th century, when it was the concert and show destination. Today it continues to be at the forefront of popular culture, hosting performances by leading musicians, circus acts, ballet and shows, as well as occasional sports events such as kickboxing. *Rua das Portas de Santo Antão.* ☎ *21-324-080. Tickets 10€– 35€. www.coliseulisboa.pt. Metro: Rossio, Restauradores. Map p 128.*

★★★ Grande e Pequeno Auditorio: Calouste Gulbenkian Foundation SALDANHA   The

Gulbenkian Choir and Gulbenkian Orchestra are both respected worldwide for their performances. Part of the Calouste Gulbenkian Foundation, the most prestigious cultural organization in Portugal, they perform an annual season of concerts in the large and small auditoriums at the foundation's headquarters. There's also an annual program of visiting international orchestras. *Avenida da Berna.* ☎ *21-782-370. Tickets 18€–60€. www.musica. gulbenkian.pt. Metro: São Sebastião, Praça de Espanha. Map p 127.*

★★★ Pavilhão Atlântico

PARQUE DAS NACOES   Built as part of the Expo '98 project in Parque das Nações, this eye-catching large pavilion looks like a squashed bubble. It hosts major sporting events and concerts by the most renowned national and international stars, as well as congresses and other events. *Rossio dos Olivais.* ☎ *21-891-8409. Tickets 12€–50€. www.pavilhao atlantico.pt. Metro: Oriente.*

★★★ Teatro Nacional de São Carlos BAIRRO ALTO   Built in the

Chiado to replace the former opera house destroyed in the 1755 earthquake, this theater boasts a grand neo-classical façade and a sumptuous

The Gulbenkian Orchestra.

rococo interior. Its calendar includes its own opera productions, an annual season of concerts by the Orquesta Sinfónica Portuguesa (some of the season takes place at the CCB above), and a few contemporary theater and ballet productions. *Rua de Serpa Pinto, 9.* ☎ *21-325-3045. Tickets 25€–400€. www.saocarlos.pt. Metro: Baixa-Chiado. Map p 128.*

Dance

★★★ Centro Cultural de Belém BELEM See Concert venues above.

★★★ Teatro Nacional de São Carlos BAIRRO ALTO See Concert venues above.

★★ Teatro Camões PARQUE DAS NACOES Home to the Companhia Nacional de Bailado (National Ballet Company) since 2003, and a major performance space with various productions during each season. *Paseo Neptuno.* ☎ *21-892-3470. www. cnb.pt. Metro: Oriente.*

Film

Cinema Londres CAMPO PEQUENO Now owned by Castello Lopes Cinemas, this small moviehouse has two screens and is an intimate alternative to the large moviehouses in the shopping centers. *Avenida Roma, 7A.* ☎ *21-840-1313. Tickets 6€. Metro: Campo Pequeno, Roma, Areeiro. Map p 127.*

★★ Cinema de São Jorge AVENIDA This was the biggest moviehouse in Portugal, when it opened in the 1950s, and was state of the art with the latest gadgets such as air-conditioning. Today it has been renovated and hosts premiers, festivals, and other major events. *Avenida da Liberdade, 174.* ☎ *21-310-3402. www.egeac.pt. Tickets various Metro: Avenida. Map p 128.*

★★ Cinemateca AVENIDA More than a cinema, this is a movie museum, archive, exhibition center and movie bookshop In an elegant 19th-century building. It has recently been renovated and hosts two underground movies each month. *Rua Barata Salgueiro, 39.* ☎ *21-359-6200. www.cinemateca.pt. Tickets 2.5€. Metro: Avenida, Rato. Map p 128.*

★★ Lusomundo AMOREIRAS/ BENFINCA/PARQUE DAS NACOES These multiplex moviehouses in Amoreiras, Colombo, and Vasco da Gama shopping centers screen the latest blockbuster releases mostly in the original language with subtitles

Opera fans should check out the productions at Teatro Nacional São Carlos.

in Portuguese. *Amoreiras Shopping, Avenida Engenheiro Duarte Pacheco.* ☎ *21-383-1275. Metro: Rato. Map p 128.*

Colombo Shopping, Avenida Avenida Lusiada. ☎ *21-711-322. Metro: Colegio Militar.*

Vasco da Gama Shopping, Avenida Dom João II. ☎ *21-892-2280. Metro: Rato.*

UCI Cinemas SALDANHA   This cinema in El Corte Inglés department store in Saldanha is a multiplex showing the latest releases with Portuguese subtitles. It's also the largest cinema in the city with 14 screens. *Avenida Antonio Augista Aguiar.* ☎ *707-232-221. Metro: Saldanha. Map p 127.*

Fringe Arts Centers

★ **Chapitô** ALFAMA   This is a cultural center with a restaurant, bar, café, theater, and performance arts school. Located in the heart of the Alfama, you'll see *fado*, theatre, circus, films and more. Just drop in and see what's on or even join a workshop. *Costa do Castelo, 1-7.* ☎ *21-885-5550. www.chapito.org. Tram: 28. Map p 128.*

★★ **Culturgest** CAMPO PEQUENO This multiarts venue hosts a variety of cutting-edge exhibitions, workshops, theatrical performances, and contemporary dance. *Rua Arco do Cego.* ☎ *21-790-5155. www.culturgest.pt. Metro: Campo Pequeno. Map p 127.*

Spectator Sports

★★★ **Estádio da Luz** BENFICA Home to SL Benfica, one of Portugal's premier soccer clubs, it is known to fans as *El Catedral*. If you look early enough you can buy tickets online, a sight to see, not just for the game, but for the ceremony beforehand, when a vulture flies from the top of the stadium to its handler

Chapitô is located in the heart of the Alfama.

on the pitch. There's also a museum here, telling the club's history, tours of the stadium, and a mega-shop full of Benfica kit. *Avenida Lusiada. Tickets start at 10€. www.slbenfica.pt. Tour & museum daily 5€–10€. Metro: Colegio Militar. Map p 128.*

★ **Estádio José de Alvalade** SANTS   Home to Lisbon's second soccer team, Sporting Clube de Portugal. You can take a tour of the stadium or visit Mundo Sporting, a museum on the history of the club. *Almeida das Linhas de Torres.* ☎ *707-204-444. Tickets start at 10€. www.sporting.pt. Admission 5€–5€. Metro: Campo Grande. Map p 127.*

★ **Estádio Nacional** OEIRAS Also known as Estádio do Jamor, this is Portugal's national soccer ground and hosts the *Taça de Portugal,* the Portuguese Cup. Among Glaswegians it is more renowned though for hosting the 1967 European Cup Final, when Celtic beat Inter Milan 2–1. Whenever Celtic play in Lisbon, fans still make the pilgrimage to relive their team's most glorious moment. *Complex Desportivo do Jamor, Praça da Maratona.* ☎ *21-419-7241.*

Advance Tickets & Listings

Turismo de Lisboa publishes a monthly guide called *Follow Me Lisboa*, which is available at the Lisbon Welcome Center and at many hotels and bars. As well as pages on the latest concerts, theater, festivals and other events, it has listings and articles on restaurants, bars, attractions and cultural venues. Also look out for A-Guia's free listing magazine *Lisboa No Bolsa* or browse Sapo's online listings (cultura.sapo.pt). There are several online ticket booking services, including TicketLine (☎ 707-234-234; www.ticketline.pt) and Plateia (☎ 21-434-6304; www.plateia.iol.pt). You can also buy tickets from FNAC (☎ 760-309-330; www.fnac.pt (click on "Espectáculos")) or buy them in person from any of their stores (see p 84).

Tickets start at 10€. Train Oeiras. Map p 127.

★★★ Pavilhão Atlântico
PARQUE DAS NACOES   See Concert venues above.

Theater
★★★ Teatro Nacional de Dona Maria II
BAIXA   This theater dominates the north side of Rossio Square with its grand neo-classical façade. Originally built in the 19th century, it suffered a devastating fire in the 1960s and had to be completely reconstructed. It presents a program of both national and international plays, but they are all performed in Portuguese. *Praça Dom Pedro IV.* ☎ *21-325-0827. www.teatro-dmaria.pt. Metro: Rossio, Restauradores. Map p 128.*

Multi-arts venue Culturgest.

★ Teatro São Luiz
CHIADO Once the hub of the society set, it has also seen the rise of many Portuguese stars of the stage, and *fado* diva Amália Rodrigues even performed here in 1980. It presents a mixed program of dance, theater and music. *Rua António Maria Cardoso, 54.* ☎ *21-325-7650. Metro: Baixa-Chiado. Map p 128.*

★ Teatro Tivoli
AVENIDA   This theater started out as a cinema in the 1920s but theatrical productions slowly crept in along with musicals and ballet. Today it is still one of the most striking neo-classical buildings in the Avenida da Liberdade and hosts a mixed program of performances for adults and kids, as well as the occasional film festival. *Avenida da Liberdade, 182.* ☎ *21-357-2025. www.teatro-tivoli.com. Metro: Restauradores, Avenida. Map p 128.*

★ Teatro Politeama
BAIXA Located opposite the Coliseu dos Recreios, this grand old theater presents major musicals in Portuguese. *Rua das Portas de Santo Antão, 109.* ☎ *21-324-500. www.teatropoliteama.net. Ticket prices vary. Metro: Restauradores. Map p 128.* ●

Lodging **Best Bets**

Best **Historic Hotel**
★★★ Palácio Belmonte $$$$$
Páteo Dom Fradique, 14 (p 146)

Best **Palace Hotel**
★★★ Pestana Palace Hotel $$$$
Rua Jau, 54 (p 146)

Best **Boutique Hotel**
★★★ Hotel Bairro Alto
$$$$–$$$$$ *c/ de la Marina,
19–21 (p 140)*

Best **New Hotel**
★★ Jerónimos 8 $$$ *Rua dos
Jerónimos 5 (p 143)*

Best **City Center Location**
★★★ Hotel Avenida Palace $$$$
R 1° de Dezembro, 123 (p 141)

Best **Luxury City Hotel**
★★★ Sofitel $$$–$$$$ *Avenida da
Liberdade, 127 (p 147)*

Best **Views**
★★★ Albergaria Senhora do
Monte $$ *Calçada do Monte, 39
(p 140)*

Best **Hideaway**
★★★ York House Hotel $$$ *Rua
das Janelas Verdes, 32 (p 148)*

Best for **Parks**
★ Avenida Park Residence $
Avenida Sidónia Pais, 6 (p 140)

Best for **Business**
★★ VIP Executive Barcelona $$
Rua Laura Alves, 10 (p 148)

Best for **Families**
★★ Mercure Lisboa $$ *Avenida
José Malhoa, 1684 (p 146)*

Best **Facilities**
★★ Corinthia Lisboa Hotel $$–$$$
*Avenida Columbano Bordalo
Pinheiro, 105 (p 140)*

Best **Residencial**
★ Residencial Dom Sancho I $
Avenida da Liberdade, 202 (p 147)

Best **on a Budget**
★ Residencial Florescente $ *Rua
das Portas de Santo Antão, 99
(p 147)*

Best **Spa Pampering**
★★★ Lapa Palace Hotel $$$$
Rua Pau da Bandeira, 4. (p 143)

Best Boutique Hotel, the Hotel Bairro Alto.

Belém/Alcântara Lodging

Jeronimos 8 **1**

Pestana Palace Hotel **2**

Parque das Nações Lodging

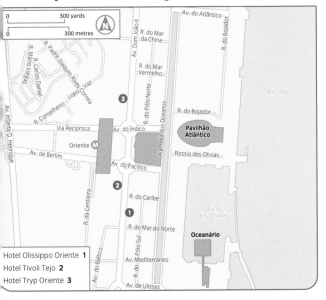

Hotel Olissippo Oriente **1**

Hotel Tivoli Tejo **2**

Hotel Tryp Oriente **3**

City Center Lodging

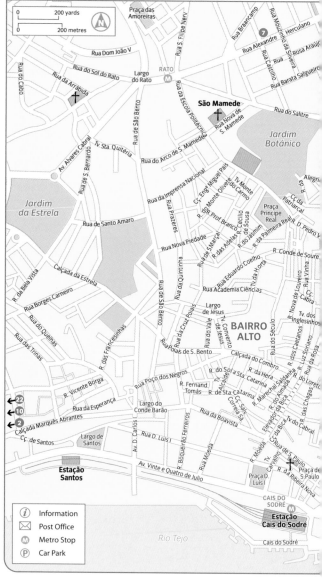

0 ——— 200 yards
0 ——— 200 metres

Praça das Amoreiras

Rua Dom João V

Rua do Sol do Rato

Largo do Rato   RATO Ⓜ

Rua do Cabo

Rua da Arrábida

Av. Álvares Cabral

Tv. Sta. Quitéria

Rua de S. Bernardo

Rua de São Bento

Rua da Escola Politécnica

São Mamede †

Rua Nova de S. Mamede

Rua do Arco de S. Mamede

Rua do Salitre

Rua Braancamp

Rua Mouzinho da Silveira

Rua Alexandre Herculano

Rua Castilho

Rua Rosa Araújo

Rua Barata Salgueiro

Rua S. Filipe Nery

❼

Jardim Botânico

Jardim da Estrela

Rua de Santo Amaro

Rua da Imprensa Nacional

Rua Prazeres

CC. Eng.º Miguel País

R. D.ª Monte Olivete

Tv. Monte do Carmo

R.ª Prof Branco

R.ª Cecílio de Sousa

Rua Nova Piedade

Rua de S.ª Marçal

R. das Adelas

R. do Jasmim

R. da Palmeira

R. D. Pedro V

Praça Príncipe Real

CC. da Patriarcal

Alegria

Ep.ª

R. Conde de Soure

Rua da Quintinha

Rua Eduardo Coelho

Tv. da Horta

R. Nova do Loureiro

Rua Vinha

CC. da Cabra

Rua Académia Ciências

Largo de Jesus

Tv. Convento de Jesus

BAIRRO ALTO

Rua do Século

R. dos Caetanos

Tv. dos Inglesinhos

Rua de São Bento

Rua da Cruz Poiais

Rua do Vale

Poias de S. Bento

Calçada do Combro

R. do Sol à Sta. Catarina

R. da Hera

R. dos Mastros

Rua de S. Paulo

R. da Rosa

R. da Bela Vista

Rua Borges Carneiro

Calçada da Estrela

Rua do Quelhas

Rua das Trinas

R. das Francesinhas

R. Vicente Borga

Rua Poço dos Negros

R. Fernand. Tomás

R. de Sta. Catarina

R. Saraiva Carvalho

Correia

Rua da Boavista

R. Marechal Saldanha

Elevador da Bica

Tv. da Bica

R. da Bica

Tv. do Cabral

R. do Loreto

R. Luz Soriano

Rua da Esperança

Largo do Conde Barão

Rua Moeda

R. da Boavista

Tv. Cavalinho

Praça de S. Paulo

† R. da Ribeira Nova

Praça D. Luis I

Av. D. Carlos

Rua D. Luís I

R. Boqueirão Ferreiros

Rua Moeda

Av. Vinte e Quatro de Julho

←22
←10
←2

Calçada Marquês Abrantes

CC. de Santos

Largo de Santos

Estação Santos

CAIS DO SODRÉ

Estação Cais do Sodré Ⓜ

Cais do Sodré

Rio Tejo

ⓘ Information
⊠ Post Office
Ⓜ Metro Stop
Ⓟ Car Park

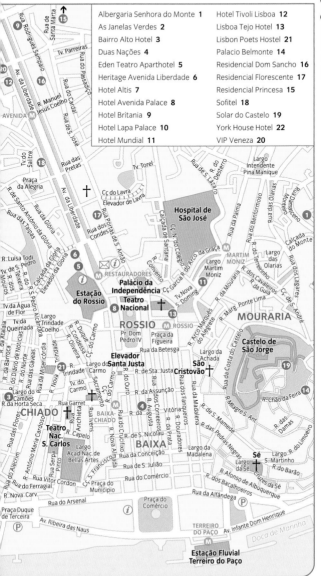

Albergaria Senhora do Monte **1**
As Janelas Verdes **2**
Bairro Alto Hotel **3**
Duas Nações **4**
Eden Teatro Aparthotel **5**
Heritage Avenida Liberdade **6**
Hotel Altis **7**
Hotel Avenida Palace **8**
Hotel Britania **9**
Hotel Lapa Palace **10**
Hotel Mundial **11**
Hotel Tivoli Lisboa **12**
Lisboa Tejo Hotel **13**
Lisbon Poets Hostel **21**
Palacio Belmonte **14**
Residencial Dom Sancho **16**
Residencial Florescente **17**
Residencial Princesa **15**
Sofitel **18**
Solar do Castelo **19**
York House Hotel **22**
VIP Veneza **20**

North of Center Lodging

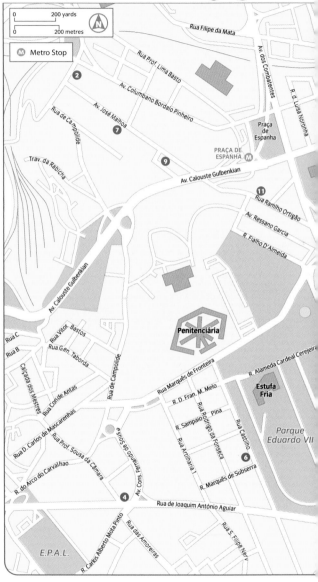

0 — 200 yards
0 — 200 metres

Ⓜ Metro Stop

Rua Filipe da Mata

Av. dos Combatentes

Rua Prof. Lima Basto

R. d. Luísa Noronha

2

Av. Columbano Bordalo Pinheiro

Av. José Malhoa

Rua de Campolide

7

Praça de Espanha

Trav. da Rabicha

9

PRAÇA DE ESPANHA Ⓜ

Av. Calouste Gulbenkian

11

Rua Ramilho Ortigão

Av. Ressano Garcia

R. Fialho D'Almeida

Av. Calouste Gulbenkian

Rua C

Rua B

Rua Vítor Bastos

Rua Gen. Taborda

Calçada dos Mestres

Rua Conde Antas

Rua de Campolide

Penitenciária

Rua Marquês de Fronteira

R. Alameda Cardeal Cerejeira

R. D. Fran. M. Melo

R. Sampaio Pina

Rua Rodrigo da Fonseca

Estufa Fria

Rua D. Carlos de Mascarenhas

Rua Prof. Sousa da Câmara

R. do Arco do Carvalhao

Av. Cons. Fernando Sousa

Rua Artilharia 1

Rua Castilho

6

Parque Eduardo VII

R. Marquês de Subserra

4

Rua de Joaquim António Aguiar

R. Carlos Alberto Mota Pinto

Rua das Amoreiras

Rua S. Filipe Nery

E.P.A.L.

Avenida Park Residence **1**
Corinthia Lisboa Hotel **2**
Holiday Inn **3**
Hotel Dom Pedro **4**
Hotel Fenix **5**
Hotel Zenit **8**
Mercure Lisboa **7**
Meridien Park Atlantic **6**
Novotel **9**
Real Palácio Hotel **10**
Real Residencia Suite Hotel **11**
VIP Executive Barcelona **12**

Lisbon Lodging **A to Z**

★★ **Albergaria Senhora do Monte** ALFAMA
Located on the slopes of the Alfama, this guesthouse is clean and basic but some of the rooms have large terraces with great views down over the Tagus River. *Calçada do Monte, 39.* ☎ *21-886-6002. 28 units. Doubles 98€–120€. AE, MC, V. Tram: 28. Map p 137.*

★★★ **As Janelas Verdes** SANTOS
A boutique hotel in a historic 18th-century house next door to the Ancient Art Museum and reputedly where Portuguese writer Eça de Queiros lived in the 19th century. Its interior is sleek and classy, with Portuguese furnishings complementing the older architecture. The garden is a quiet shaded retreat and there's a library with a terrace overlooking the river. *Rua das Janelas Verdes, 47.* ☎ *21-396-8143. www.heritage.pt. 29 units. Doubles 170€–320€. AE, DC, MC, V. Tram: 15, 25. Map p 137.*

★ **Avenida Park Residence** SAO SEBASTIAO
Recently renovated, some of the rooms in this guesthouse look directly over Parque Eduardo VII. Portuguese touches such as traditional tiles in the bathroom blend well with modern and bright public spaces downstairs. *Avenida Sidónia Pais, 6.* ☎ *21-353-2181. www.avenidapark. com. 40 units. Doubles 55€. AE, DC, MC, V. Metro: Marquês de Pombal. Map p 139.*

★★★ **Bairro Alto Hotel** BAIRRO ALTO
This boutique hotel has only been open a few years and has a growing reputation. In a restored 18th-century building, it deftly combines classic Portuguese décor with contemporary touches, including art and photographs by local artists. There's also a restaurant, bar, gym and wellness center, plus the bonus of Lisbon nightlife on your doorstep. *Praça Luís de Camões, 2.* ☎ *21-340-8288. www.bairroaltohotel.com. 55 units. Doubles 270€–450€. AE, MC, V. Metro: Baixa-Chiado. Tram: 28. Map p 137.*

★★ **kids Corinthia Lisboa Hotel** CAMPOLIDE
Close to Lisbon Zoo and with views of the 18th-century aqueduct from the upper floors, this huge hotel has facilities to match. It's regularly used for congresses but it also caters for leisure guests with two restaurants, bar, outdoor pool and fitness center, plus a babysitting service. *Avenida Columbano Bordalo Pinheiro, 105.* ☎ *21-723-6363. www.corinthia hotels.com. 518 units. Doubles 99€–285€. AE, DC, MC, V. Metro: Praça de Espanha. Map p 139.*

★ **Duas Nações** BAIXA
A rarity, this B&B is located right in the heart of the Baixa. The building is old and the rooms are basic and not all have en suite bathrooms,

Hotel Bairro Alto.

The Art Deco Eden Teatro Aparthotel.

but most have windows opening onto the vibrant streets outside, Beware, although it quietens down at night, noises echo through these grid-like streets. *Rua dos Condes de Monsanto, 2.* ☎ *21-886-6182. www.duasnacoes.com. 51 units. Doubles 35€–110€. AE, DC, MC, V. Tram: 15, 28. Metro: Rossio. Map p 137.*

★★ Eden Teatro Aparthotel

BAIXA   This stylish Art Deco building was once a theater but was transformed into an aparthotel a few years ago. Right on the Praça dos Restauradores, its studios and apartments face onto an atrium and there's a terrace with huge city views. *Praça dos Restauradores, 24.* ☎ *21-321-6600. www.viphotels.com. 134 units. Doubles 90€–128€. MC, V. Elevador da Glória. Metro: Restauradores. Map p 137.*

★★★ Heritage Avenida Liberdade

RESTAURADORES   Opened in 2006, a small, modern boutique hotel in a restored 18th-century property. Stylishly designed by Portuguese architect Miguel Câncio Martins (whose other projects include the Buddha Bar in Paris and Man Ray in New York), there are comfortable public spaces, a luxury spa, and contemporary neutral

rooms with city center views. *Avenida da Liberdade, 28.* ☎ *21-340-4040. www.heritage.pt. 42 units. Doubles 206€–253€. AE, DC, MC, V. Metro: Restauradores, Avenida. Map p 137.*

★ Holiday Inn SALDANHA

Located in the business district, just minutes from the metro station, facilities range from the roof-top pool and mini-gym to a buffet restaurant and large lobby bar. It's very reasonable but do reserve in advance. *Avenida António José de Almeida, 28-A.* ☎ *21-004-4000. www.ichotelsgroup.com. 169 units. Doubles 80€–124€. AE, DC, MC, V. Metro: Saldanha. Map p 139.*

★★ Hotel Altis RATO   At this top

Lisbon hotel, facilities and comfort beat stylistic statements hands down. What stands out are the location, just off the Avenida da Liberdade, the pool and beauty parlor, and the superb roof-top views from its restaurant-grill D. Fernando. *Rua Castilho, 11.* ☎ *21-310-6000. www. altishotels.com. 303 units. Doubles 165€–250€. AE, DC, MC, V. Metro: Rato, Avenida. Map p 137.*

★★ Hotel Avenida Palace

ROSSIO   Designed by the architect of Rossio Station, this Belle Époque

Types of Lodging

In Portugal, all accommodation is classified by a starring system within its category with 5 at the top and 1 at the budget end. Hotels can range from modern towers to boutique hotels. A number of hotels in Lisbon are located in former palaces, usually indicated in the title. Pousadas are located in converted historic buildings; the nearest ones to Lisbon are in Queluz and Setúbal, For more information, see www.pousadas.pt (☎ 21-844-2001). Most hotels in Portugal serve breakfast, but do check this at the time of booking. Prices are generally quoted per room rather than per person. There are various kinds of B&B/ boarding houses, called solar, albergaria, pensão, and residencial. These are often in more traditional buildings with Portuguese tiles. A pensão or residencial is usually a cheaper option. There are also a number of private hostels in Lisbon with both shared and individual rooms.

palace-hotel dates back to 1892. Recent restorations have enhanced the style and décor of the period, with an English-style dark-wood bar, and the Palace Lounge is a gem with its 19th-century glass ceiling, but there are also modern comforts here from AC to Wi-Fi. *R 1° de Dezembro, 123.* ☎ *21-321-8100. www.hotel-avenida-palace.com. 82 units. Doubles 180€–425€. AE, MC, V. Metro: Rossio, Restauradores. Map p 137.*

★★ **Hotel Britania** ANJOS Built in the 1940s by famed Portuguese architect Cassiano Branco, this just oozes with Art Deco style. It has been restored since then, but the style remains intact, mixed with a helping of contemporary design. Its location on a quiet road off the Avenida da Liberdade means you can escape the city traffic and retreat to the bar and open fire. *Rua Rodrigues Sampaio, 17.* ☎ *21-315-5016.*

The pool and gardens at Hotel Lapa Palace.

Hotel Mundial has great views of the city.

www.heritage.pt. 30 units. Doubles 244€–326€. AE, DC, MC, V. Metro: Avenida. Map p 137.

★★★ **Hotel Dom Pedro** AMOR-EIRAS   With its blue-mirrored glass exterior, this high-rise hotel reflects the clouds and the Amoreiras shopping center opposite. Inside you can sink into deep lobby sofas after a day's sightseeing, retreat to the traditional comfort of your room, catch up on e-mail, or enjoy dinner in its Italian restaurant. *Avenida Eng. Duarte Pacheco 24.* ☎ 21-330-0541. www.dompedro.com. 263 units. Doubles 130€–2647€. AE, MC, V. Metro: Rato. Map p 139.

★★ **Hotel Fénix** ALFAMA   You can't miss this hotel on the edge of Praça Marquês de Pombal with its name in lights emblazoned across the top. At the heart of Lisbon's road network, business, leisure and culture activities are within easy reach and catered for in the hotel. You can retreat to the vast lounges inside or the palm-filled atrium garden. *Praça Marquês de Pombal, 8.* ☎ 21-386-2121. www.hoteisfenix.com. 192 units. Doubles 120€–220€. AE, DC, MC, V. Metro: Marquês de Pombal. Map p 139.

★★ **Hotel Jerónimos 8** BELEM   This contemporary hotel opened in 2007 replacing the former Hotel da Torre and offering a rare opportunity to stay in Belém. There's a retro-trendy bar on the ground floor and the contemporary rooms lead onto a decked terrace where you can sit out in the evening. *Rua dos Jerónimos.* ☎ 21 360 0900. www.almeidahotels.com. 65 units. Doubles 180€–210€. AE, DC, MC, V. Tram: 15. Map p 135.

★★★ **Hotel Lapa Palace** LAPA   A city oasis where you can indulge in luxurious spa treatments, lie out by the pool in the lush gardens, join the ladies of Lisbon for afternoon tea, and enjoy intimate dining the Cipriani restaurant. Choose from rooms in the palace, garden or villa wings, or splash out on the tower room with outdoor terrace and 360 degree views. *Rua Pau da Bandeira, 4.* ☎ 21-330-0541. www.lapapalace.com. 109 units. Doubles 270€–675€. AE, MC, V. Tram: 15. Map p 137.

★★ **Hotel Mundial** BAIXA   Just a few minutes from Rossio Square, this large hotel has comfortable rooms and substantial breakfasts. It prides itself on its eating and drinking facilities, which also include a bar and substantial wine cellar and the Varanda de Lisboa restaurant with panoramic views. *Praça Martim Moniz.* ☎ 21-884-2000. www.hotel-mundial.com. 350 units. Doubles 125€–300€. AE, DC, MC, V. Tram: 12, 28. Metro: Martim Moniz. Map p 137.

★★ **Hotel Olissippo Oriente** PARQUE DAS NACOES   The modern, bright, white of the exterior is reflected inside with crisp white bed linen and contrasting scatter cushions for the stylish, contemporary touch. There's a similar feel throughout the hotel's bars and public areas, and it is close to Lisbon's FIL conference center. *Avenida Dom João II.* ☎ 21-892-9100. www.olissippohotels.com. 182 units. Doubles 134€–400€. AE, DC, MC, V. Metro: Oriente. Map p 135.

Hotel Olissippo Oriente.

★★★ Hotel Tivoli Lisboa

AVENIDA If you want luxury and comfort in the city center, this is popular with executives and tourists on short breaks. The décor is traditional, its restaurants are smart, one with a roof terrace, plus there's a piano bar and an outdoor pool in a leafy garden. *Avenida da Liberdade, 185.* ☎ *21-319-8900. www.tivolihotels. com. 329 units. Doubles 149€–347€. AE, DC, MC, V. Metro: Avenida, Restauradores. Map p 137.*

★★ Hotel Tivoli Tejo PARQUE

DAS NACOES Suitable for both business trips and family stays, this contemporary hotel in the heart of Parque das Nações is clean and comfortable. The pool and health club will keep both kids and adults happy, along with its ample buffet breakfast, restaurants, parking, and Wi-Fi. For quieter rooms, request accommodation on the upper floors. *Avenida Dom João II.* ☎ *21-891-5100. www.tivolihotels. com. 279 units. Doubles 105€–210€. AE, MC, V. Metro: Oriente. Map p 135.*

★★ Hotel Tryp Oriente PARQUE

DAS NACOES One of just a handful of places to stay in this part of town, this is a high-rise hotel with views across the park. Clean and contemporary with its own restaurant and bar, and offers modern comfort, Wi-Fi and easy access to transport,

shopping and the airport. *Avenida Dom João II.* ☎ *21-893-000. www. solmelia.com. 207 units. 95€–106€. AE, DC, MC, V. Metro: Oriente. Map p 135.*

★★★ Le Meridien Park Atlantic Lisboa PARQUE

An 18-story hotel looking over the Parque Eduardo VII, this is a large hotel but its plush soft furnishings give it a cozy feel. Close to the business district but within easy reach of the metro, the park's sport and leisure (p 92) and city center attractions. Guest rooms are contemporary, plus there's a health club, restaurant, bar and babysitting service. *Rua Castilho, 149.* ☎ *21-381-8700. www.lemeridien.com/ lisbon. 331 units. Doubles 127€– 220€. AE, MC, V. Metro: Pombal. Map p 139.*

★ Lisboa Camping If you fancy

something a little more out in the open, there's this campsite in the Parque Florestal de Monsanto with either space to pitch a tent or furnished chalets for 2 to 6 people. There's easy access to the city center via the Lisbon–Cascais motorway plus the campsite has pools, a restaurant, a shop, washing facilities, and a kids' play area. *Estrada da Circunvalação.* ☎ *21-762-3100. www.lisboacamping.com. Tents 4.10€–7€; caravans 5€–9€; 2-person chalet 10€–65€.*

Reserving Accommodation

To get the best deals, reserve ahead, particularly if going during the summer months from June to September. June is particularly busy because of Lisbon's festivities. Hotels also fill up around New Year. There are various options for reserving lodging online, including Expedia (www.expedia.com) or the comprehensive Portuguese Maisturismo (www.maisturismo.com). There are some hostels on these websites, otherwise try www.hostels.com or www.lisbon hostels.com.

If arriving in Lisbon without lodging, either ask at the Lisbon Welcome Center (see p 171) or look for a residencial or pensão in the streets around Rossío Square and off Avenida da Liberdade. If you'd rather stay in a hotel and the city center options are booked out, try the business district, where the hotels can be surprisingly good value and just a metro ride away.

★ **Lisboa Tejo Hotel** BAIXA The reception in this Baixa hotel is a funky mix of bare brick and contemporary wood-and-glass bar, with blue accents matching the exterior, corridors and basic but comfortable rooms. Downstairs in the bookish breakfast room you can help yourself to the cereals, fresh fruit, and hot eggs first thing. *Rua dos Condes de Monsanto, 2.* ☎ *21-886-6182. www.evidencia hoteis.com. 51 units. Doubles 85€– 120€. AE, DC, MC, V. Tram: 15, 28. Metro: Rossio. Map p 137.*

★ **Lisbon Poets Hostel** BAIRRO ALTO Budget option in the heart of the Bairro Alto with double rooms and dormitories. The bunks are tightly packed in some rooms but it's clean with wooden floors and typical Portuguese tiles on the walls. There's also kitchen facilities, laundry, living room, mini-bar, and free breakfast. *Rua do Duque, 41.* ☎ *21-346-1058. www.lisbonpoets hotel.com. Shared rooms, per person 18€–20€; double room 40€–44€. Map p 137.*

Lisbon Poets Hostel.

★★ **kids** **Mercure Lisboa** CAMPOLIDE   This hotel might not be downtown, but it's just a 10-minute walk from Lisbon Zoo and the Parque Florestal de Monsanto, and the metro is minutes away. There's a pool, open year round, a restaurant and a bar. *Avenida José Malhoa, 1684.* ☎ *21-720-8000. www.mercure.com. 104 units. Doubles 85€–120€. AE, DC, MC, V. Metro: Campolilde. Map p 139.*

★ **Hotel Zenit** SALDANHA   This hotel occupies a rather striking 19th-century corner building, painted blue and white, highlighting its original features. Inside, it's smart and contemporary with a buffet breakfast and international dinner menu in its restaurant. *Avenida 5 de Octubro, 11.* ☎ *21-310-2200. www.zenithoteles.com. 86 units. Doubles 80€–110€. AE, MC, V. Metro: Saldanha. Map p 139.*

★ **kids** **Novotel.** CAMPOLIDE   Large, modern and comfortable, this renowned hotel is between Lisbon Zoo and the Gulbenkian Museum. It's ideal for families as there's an outdoor pool (you can order food there), and play areas for kids both inside and outside the

A variety of hotels can be found near the Avenida da Liberdade.

hotel. *Avenida José de Malhoa, 1-1A.* ☎ *21-330-0541. www.novotel.com. 249 units. Doubles 79€–170€. AE, DC, MC, V. Metro: Praça de Espanha. Map p 139.*

★★★ **Palácio Belmonte** ALFAMA   A romantic hideaway just outside the walls of the Castelo de São Jorge, this 15th-century palace-hotel has 10 unique suites, individually dressed with Portuguese tiles, antiques and pieces of art, and named after historic Portuguese personalities from writers and travelers to Jesuits and philosophers. Its library has around 4,000 tomes and there's a black-marble pool. *Páteo Dom Fradique, 14.* ☎ *21-881-6609. www.palaciobelmonte.com. 10 units. Suites 400€–700€. AE, DC, MC, V. Tram: 28. Map p 137.*

★ **Pensão Residencial Princesa** ARROIOS   To the east of the Avenida da Liberdade, this B&B-style accommodation is basic, clean and comfortable and real value for money. Located off the main thoroughfare, this is a quieter choice. *Rua Gomes Freire, 130.* ☎ *21-319-3070. www.residencial-princesa.com. 47 units. Doubles 51€–75€. AE, DC, MC, V. Metro: Avenida. Map p 137.*

★★★ **Pestana Palace Hotel** ALCANTARA   This sets a tone of luxury from the moment the uniformed doorman opens the car door to the grand high-ceilinged accommodation complete with gilt-edged cornices. It has marble floors, sweeping stairs, chandeliers, antiques, painted ceilings, lush tropical gardens, and two pools. There are also two restaurants and a bar with views across the grounds. *Rua Jau, 54.* ☎ *21-361-5600. www.pestana.com. 190 units. Doubles 240€–260€. AE, DC, MC, V. Tram: 15. Map p 135.*

★★ **kids** **Real Palácio Hotel** PARQUE   A 17th-century former palace and an adjacent building

Real Residencia Suite.

have been combined to create this quality hotel. Large and pink on the outside, the interior is quite traditional and functional, plus there's a gym and sauna, but where it excels is its facilities for kids, which include kids' furniture and menus, and babysitting. *Rua Tomás Ribeiro, 115.* ☎ *21-319-9500. www.hoteisreal. com. 147 units. Doubles 125€–260€. AE, MC, V. Metro: Parque. Map p 139.*

★★★ Real Residencia Suite Hotel PARQUE Cheaper than its sister, Real Palacio Hotel, this aparthotel has 1- and 2-bed suites for less money and it offers kids' furniture, menus, and babysitting; you can still use the gym facilities at the sister hotel. The apartments have equipped kitchenettes and there's a restaurant/café/bar. *Rua Ramalho Ortigão, 41.* ☎ *21-382-2900. www.hoteisreal.com. 24 units. Doubles 120€. AE, MC, V. Metro: São Sebastião. Map p 139.*

★ Residencial Dom Sancho I AVENIDA In an 18th-century building on the Avenida da Liberdade, this B&B has a local flavor with white-washed walls, Portuguese antique-style furnishings, and *azulejos* (tiled) panels on the walls. They do a continental buffet breakfast with bread, cheeses and

jams. *Avenida da Liberdade, 202.* ☎ *21-354-8042. www.domsancho. com. 40 units. Doubles 80€–100€. AE, MC, V. Metro: Avenida, Restauradores. Map p 137.*

★ Residencial Florescente BAIXA This B&B is located on a lively street buzzing with restaurants. Inside it's bright, clean and typically Portuguese, with wall tiles and even a shop selling crafts. Rooms are basic and, as this is a busy street for socializing, noise can be an issue, but there are some with 3 beds and for such a central location it's not expensive. *Rua das Portas de Santo Antão, 99.* ☎ *21-342-6609. www.residencial florescente.com. 68 units. Doubles 45€–65€. AE, DC, MC, V. Metro: Rossio, Restauradores. Map p 137.*

★★★ Sofitel AVENIDA This is a luxury hotel in the heart of the tree-lined Avenida da Liberdade. You can expect an understated mix of traditional and modern décor in the guestrooms and adventurous but elegant dining in its Ad-Lib restaurant (see p 109). *Avenida da Liberdade, 127.* ☎ *21-322-8300. www.sofitel.com. 171 units. Doubles 111€–126€. AE, MC, V. Metro: Avenida. Map p 137.*

VIP Executive Barcelona Hotel.

★★★ **Solar do Castelo** ALFAMA

Within the grounds of the Castelo de São Jorge, this is believed to be on the site of the castle kitchens; there's still a medieval cistern here (don't worry, it's not for guest use). Most of the building dates to around the 18th century, but the thick stone walls really give it the feel of a castle, while the patio and pond at the back seem more colonial. The interiors have been carefully restored with a mix of antique style and contemporary furnishings. *Rua das Cozinhas, 2.* ☎ *21-880-6050. www.heritage.pt. 14 units. Doubles 310€–425€. AE, DC, MC, V. Tram: 28. Map p 137.*

★★ **VIP Executive Barcelona Hotel** ALVALADE

In the heart of Lisbon's financial district (and not far from the Calouste Gulbenkian Foundation), this hotel is modern and smart, with a bar with comfortable armchairs where you can relax over a drink. *Rua Laura Alves, 10.* ☎ *21-795-4273. www.viphotels. com. 125 units. Doubles 59€–67€. MC, V. Tram: 15, 28. Metro: Campo Pequeno. Map p 139.*

★ **VIP Veneza Hotel** AVENIDA

Handily central, this occupies a converted 19th-century palacette. You get classical-style comfort but not luxury for your money. However, it has retained some of its historic grandeur such as the wood-paneled sitting room and a few stained-glass windows. *Avenida da Liberdade, 189.* ☎ *21-352-2618. www.vip hotels.com. 37 units. Doubles 55€–62€. MC, V. Metro: Avenida, Restauradores. Map p 137.*

★★★ **York House Hotel**

ALFAMA   A boutique hotel in a 17th-century former Carmelite convent, this has décor in a mix of classical and modern chic, the rooms combining neutral and feature colored walls, clean lines, and contemporary furniture. Add the restaurant and leafy terrace, and this makes an ideal hideaway for a romantic weekend. *Rua das Janelas Verdes, 32.* ☎ *21-396-2435. www. yorkhouselisboa.com. 32 units. Doubles 150€–260€. AE, DC, MC, V. Tram: 15, 25. Map p 136.* ●

Costa do Estoril Beach Hopping

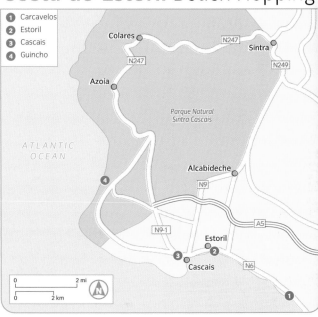

1. Carcavelos
2. Estoril
3. Cascais
4. Guincho

Colares

N247

Sintra

N247

N249

Azoia

Parque Natural
Sintra Cascais

ATLANTIC
OCEAN

Alcabideche

N9

A5

N9-1

Estoril

Cascais

N6

0   2 mi
0   2 km

One reason I find Lisbon so manageable even in the heat of summer is that it's so easy to escape for a swim in the ocean. Just a short trip out of Lisbon, the Costa do Estoril has beaches all the way along the coast, ideal for both families and surfers. Some of this selection are reachable by train (Cais do Sodré station in Lisbon), but for others you'll need a car.

Estoril Beach.

Guincho Kite Surfing.

1 ★★ Carcavelos. From Carcavelos station, it's about a 7-minute walk to the beach. Long and sandy, and overlooked by the large Forteza de São Julião da Barra (St. Julian of Barra Fortress), it's popular with surfers though during the summer, you need to surf early in the day to avoid the daytrippers. Windsurf Café on Avenida Marginal (☎ 21 457 8965) runs courses. *By train: Carcavelos station. By car: N6 coast road or A5 motorway, jct. 8.*

2 ★★ Estoril. Between Cascais and Estoril, sandy Praia de Tamariz is dotted with sunshades and is popular with families. The original 19th-century resort is nearby, with its hotels, grandiose mansions, and Estoril Casino. Between here and Carcavelos, São Pedro, São João, and Parede are all small, sandy beaches frequented by families and surfers. *By train: Parede, São Pedro, São João, Estoril stations. By car: N6 coast road or A5 motorway, jct. 8.*

3 ★★ Cascais. Cascais has various beaches, plus the added bonus of its attractions (see p 154). The fishermen bring their daily catch into Praia dos Pescadores, so head instead to the tiny, sheltered Praia de Rainha, where kids can paddle, or Praia da Conceição and Praia da Duquesa for easy access to food and drink.

4 Guincho. Exposed to the Atlantic wind and waves, this hosts major surfing competitions. I love it for the wide sand dunes and pine trees, and there are useful fish restaurants nearby. A cycle path runs from Cascais, passing the Boca do Inferno (see p 154) en route, and if you have a car, follow the coast road to the dramatic cliffs and lighthouse at Cabo da Roca, the most westerly point in mainland Europe. *By car: A5 from Lisbon, then follow signs to Guincho Beach. Estrada do Guincho from Cascais.*

Fishing boats moored opposite a beach in Cascais.

Cascais & Estoril

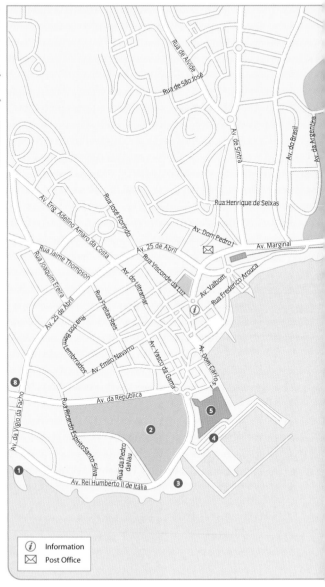

Rua de Alvide

Rua de São José

Av. de Sintra

Av. do Brasil

Av. da Argentina

Rua Henrique de Seixas

Av. Eng. Adelino Amaro da Costa

Rua José Florindo

Av. Dom Pedro I

Av. Marginal

Rua Jaime Thompson

Av. 25 de Abril

Rua Visconde da Luz

Av. Valbom

Rua Joaquim Ereira

Av. do Ultramar

Rua Frederico Arouca

Rua Freitas Reis

Rua Sargento...

Av. 25 de Abril

Av. Emílio Navarro

Av. Vasca da Gama

Av. Dom Carlos I

Rua Lembrados

❽

Av. da República

❺

Av. da Vigia da Facho

Rua Ricardo Espírito Santo Silva

❷

❹

❶

Rua da Pedro daNau

❸

Av. Rei Humberto II de Itália

ⓘ Information

✉ Post Office

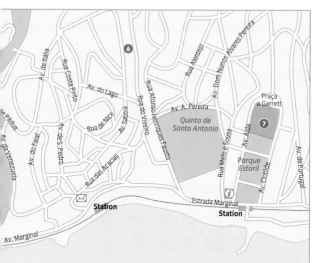

1 Boca do Inferno
2 Museu Municipal de Cascais
3 Casa de Santa Marta
4 Marina de Cascais
5 Cidadela
6 Museu da Musica
7 Estoril Casino
8 Golf courses

Cascais and Estoril have been popular with Lisboetas since the train line opened in the late 19th century and although it's been densely developed in recent decades, you can still see fanciful mansions here and there, some now museums, built by the rich (and sometimes royal exiles) former residents. Today the whole Estoril coast is one big summer playground focusing on the resorts of Estoril and Cascais.

① ★★ **Boca do Inferno.** It takes about 15 minutes to walk here from Cascais Marina past the lighthouse, and you're welcomed by a small market selling a mixture of old tat and souvenir ceramics. The 'Mouth of Hell', as it's known in English, is an ancient rock cavern, whipped away by the sea over millions of years. Look out for the plaque about occultist Aleister Crowley (1875–1947). He reputedly faked a suicide note, but in reality had skipped off to Spain to read reports about his own death. Today there are steps and railings so you can peer over the edge in relative safety. *Estrada do Guincho.*

② ★ **Museu Municipal de Cascais.** Cascais' Municipal Museum is housed in a striking gray brick and cream mock-Gothic palace-mansion, complete with misshaped windows and a tower. Close to the sea, it even has its own high-tide private pool and beach. Inside the palace combines

Museu Municipal de Cascais.

courtyards with Moorish-style fountains and tiles, with elaborate arches and large rooms with over-the-top gilt-edged mirrors, Indo-Portuguese furniture and a library of books dating back to the 17th century. At the time of writing some of the rooms have been temporarily closed for renovations, but in the meantime entrance is free. Outside are a chapel, Capela de São Sebastião, partially decorated with blue and white tiles, and a peaceful park where you can wander among the peacocks in the mini-zoo

Serene tiled chapel and gardens at the Museu Municipal de Cascais.

or stop for a coffee at the café in the center. *Palácio dos Condes de Castro Guimarães, Avenida Rei Humberto II de Itália.* ☎ *21-482-5401. Free. Open Tues–Sun 10am–5pm.*

③ ★ **Casa de Santa Marta.** On the road between the marina and Boca do Inferno, this striking colonial-style pastel-orange mansion perches on a rocky promontory overlooking the sea. At the end is the eye-catching blue-and-white 19th-century lighthouse, built on top of a recently renovated 17th-century fort. It contains an exhibition of lighthouse history and memorabilia. *Rua do Farol.* ☎ *21-481-5328 Admission X€. May–Sep Tues–Sun 10am–6pm.*

④ ★ **Marina de Cascais.** I always find marinas attractive, as they have a certain peace about them. If you're lucky, you might even see some dolphins, who like to come here to visit. But it can get busy here, with various competitions throughout the year, plus opportunities to go on sailing or fishing trips yourself (Clube Naval de Cascais ☎ 21-483-0125). Walk around the marina and you'll discover a whole row of restaurants and bars, hidden from view when you're back in the town. *Marina reception* ☎ *21-482-4899. www.marina-cascais.com. Office*

The 19th-century lighthouse.

open winter 9am–6pm; summer 9am–7pm.

⑤ ★★ **Cidadela.** Although this large fortress dominates the promontory at Cascais, all you can do at present is walk around its looming walls, although there are plans to develop it into a museum. If your Portuguese is good enough, read the note on how the current plans are going.

⑥ ★ **Museu da Musica Casa Verdades de Faria.** This small but unusual collection of Portuguese musical instruments were collected by a Corsican ethnomusicologist, Michel Giacometti (1929–90) during the 20th century and acquired from him by Mantero Belard, a local patron of the arts. The museum also houses all the assets of Portuguese

Boca do Inferno also known as the 'Mouth of Hell'.

Practical Matters: Cascais and Estoril

From Lisbon take the Avenida da Brasília past Belém and out along the N6 coast road or the A5 motorway and exit for Cascais or Estoril. Trains leave frequently (30 minutes; ☎; www.cp.pt) from Lisbon's Cais do Sodré station and take approximately 40 minutes to Cascais. The **Tourist Information Office** (☎ 21-486-8204; www.estorilcoast-tourism.com) is at Rua Visconde da Luz, 14. The tourist office offers a free bicycle lending service; just take along your passport to the booths opposite the train station and by the Cidadela (Open daily 9am–6pm).

Farol Design Hotel, (☎ 21-482-3490; www.farol.com; doubles 110€–250€), is a contemporary boutique hotel with ocean views, funky design throughout plus a pool; **Hotel Londres,** Avenida Fausto Figueiredo, 17 (☎ 21-464-8300; www.hotelondres.com; doubles 68€–90€), is a modern hotel with a pool, restaurants and just a short walk to the beach.

composer Fernando Lopes-Graça (1906–94). The house itself was designed by renowned Portuguese architect Raul Lino (1879–1974), who designed various other properties in Estoril and Cascais, including the Casa de Santa Maria (see above). He created a mansion house that displays Moorish influences in its arched windows and castellated tower. Tours of the whole house are by prior arrangement only. *Avenida*

de Saboia, 1146, Monte Estoril ☎ *21-481-5901. Open Tues–Sun 10am–1pm & 2–5pm.*

⑦ Estoril Casino. For many the casino is the highlight of their trip to Estoril. Although it's the largest casino in Europe, there's more to it than gambling rooms. I enjoyed a good dinner here, followed by a glamorous show. Men should wear a jacket and tie and women evening

Go sailing from the Marina de Cascais.

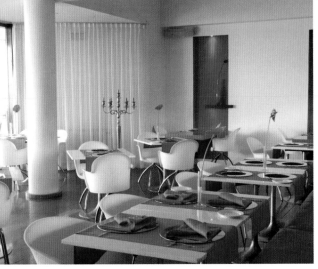

Faro Design Hotel.

dress. Upstairs there are various jewellery stores and an art gallery, and the gardens outside are an elaborate light show, with bulbs strung from tree to tree. *Praça José Teodoro dos Santos ☎ 21-466-7700. Open daily 3pm–3am.*

⑧ ★ **Golf.** There isn't enough space here for a comprehensive guide to the golf courses on the

Costa do Estoril, as there are seven 18-hole and one 9-hole course. Two of the best include: **Quinta da Marinha Oitavos Golf**, just west of Cascais and set in 110 hectares of pine woods, where you can play with the Atlantic Ocean and the Sintra Mountains as a backdrop; and **Penha Longa Atlantic**, at the foot of the Sintra hills.

Estoril Casino.

The Best Day Trips & Excursions

Sintra

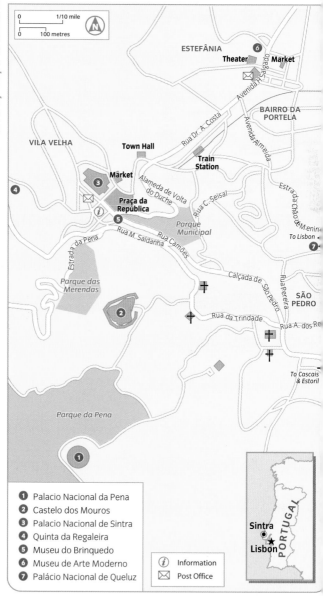

ESTEFÂNIA

Theater Market

BAIRRO DA PORTELA

Avenida H. Salgado

Avenida Almeida

Rua Dr. A. Costa

VILA VELHA

Town Hall

Train Station

Market

Alameda de Volta do Duche

Rua C. Seisal

Praça da República

Estra da Chão de Menino

To Lisbon

Parque Municipal

Estrada da Pena

Rua M. Saldanha

Rua Camões

Calçada de São Pedro

Rua Pereira

SÃO PEDRO

Parque das Merendas

Rua da Trindade

Rua A. dos Re

To Cascais & Estoril

Parque da Pena

1 Palacio Nacional da Pena
2 Castelo dos Mouros
3 Palacio Nacional de Sintra
4 Quinta da Regaleira
5 Museu do Brinquedo
6 Museu de Arte Moderno
7 Palácio Nacional de Queluz

Sintra
Lisbon
PORTUGAL

ⓘ Information
✉ Post Office

0   1/10 mile
0   100 metres

Just a short train ride from Lisbon is the UNESCO World Heritage Site of Sintra. A favorite summer retreat of the Portuguese royal family for centuries, in the 19th century it became a fantasy retreat in the wooded hills for the moneyed set. You get a comprehensive picture as you wander past spectacularly lavish mansions between the two palaces—one in the town center, the other on an airy hilltop. I like to take my time to soak up Sintra's playful curiosities and I always make a point of seeking out some queijadas, the local specialty cheese cake.

① ★★★ Palacio Nacional da Pena. Built on a hilltop, on the site of a 15th-century convent by Dom Fernando de Saxe-Coburg (king consort to Dona Maria II from 1836–1853) as a summer palace in the 19th century, this is an extraordinary over-the-top romantic fantasy. It's pure pastiche: candy-colored yellow and pink, with neo-Gothic turrets and castellations, Moorish-style horseshoe arches, walls covered in tiles, neo-Manueline motifs, mythological characters around windows and even an arch with the same diamond-shaped bricks as the Casa dos Bicos in Lisbon (p 24). It has a commanding position looking across the Sintra hills, with the outskirts of Lisbon in view, and it fits perfectly into the Pena Park's lush green grounds, which are brimming

with monuments and grottos. Only the chapel remained standing after the 1755 earthquake. Now incorporated into the palace, its retable has been restored to reveal the illustrious detail of Nicolas de Chaterenne's carved designs. *Estrada da Pena.* ☎ *21-271-0609. www.ippar.pt. Admission 4€; 2.50€ 6–17 years and seniors. Tours: 5€–11€.*

② ★ Castelo dos Mouros. From the Pena Palace you can walk downhill to the Moorish Castle, which dates to around the 9th century, when the Moors (the Muslims of north African origin) built a settlement here. Occupied alternately by the Moors and Christians, it was finally handed over voluntarily to the Portuguese after D Afonso

Palacio Nacional da Pena.

Practical Matters: Sintra

By car from Lisbon, take the IC-19 in the direction of Sintra and then either the N9 and exiting at the next junction for Sintra, or from the IC-19 take the more scenic N249 into the town. Trains leave frequently (every 15 minutes) from Lisbon's Entrecampos station, taking approximately 20 minutes to Queluz and 35 minutes to Sintra (if you want to go to the coastal resort of Maça on the tram, alight at Portela de Sintra; otherwise continue to the end of the line). The main **Posto de Turismo** is on the Praça da República, 23 (☎ 21-923-1157). A frequent **bus** connects the two palaces in Sintra, though I much prefer walking up the path to see the views unfold (the tourist office here can mark you up a map showing the route up).

Henrique's taking of Lisbon in 1147. Over time it lost its strategic importance, falling into decline from around the 14th century. There isn't a great deal left, but the battlements are impressive. If your legs can take it, climb the steps to the top of the battlements for unbeatable views up to the Pena Palace, of Sintra and the National Palace below, and across the Sintra hills all the way to the Atlantic Ocean. You can either catch the circular bus back into town (see below) but

rather than returning back to the entrance, follow the path through the woods that winds down into town. You're given a map at the castle entrance. *Parques de Sintra, Monte de Lua.* ☎ *21-910-7970. www.parquesdesintra.pt. Admission: 4.50€; 2.50€ 6–17 years and seniors. Open May–Sep 9.30am–8pm; Oct–Apr 10am–5pm.*

❸ ★ **Palacio Nacional de Sintra.** The first feature you will notice about this palace at the heart of

Palacio Nacional de Sintra.

Sintra's town centre, are its eye-catching, outsized chimneys, which you can see from the castle's turrets. In contrast to Pena Palace, this building evolved gradually over time, mostly during the 15th and 16th centuries. Although it was built on the site of a former Arab residence, The 15th-century Moorish-style tiles in the central patio and Arab room are something of a nod to the Arab residence that stood here previously. The blue-and-green geometrical designs are among my favorites as early developments of Portugal's tile culture. Other places I like to linger are the Swan Room with Manueline motifs and swans painted on the ceiling, and the Coat of Arms room. In there, the lower part is decorated with elaborate blue and white tiled scenes while the upper half, displays the painted coats of arms of Dom Manuel and 72 noble Portuguese families. *Largo Rainha Dona Amélia.* ☎ *21-910-6840. Admission 4€; 2€ 15–25 years and seniors; free under 14 years. Open daily 10am–5pm.*

Quinta da Regaleira.

❹ ★ **Quinta da Regaleira.**
You'll have to walk out of the town centre (or take the bus) to reach the Regaleira Gardens but it's worth the effort. The estate has various owners before it was given its current landscape. Constructed between 1904 and 1911 by designer Luigi Manini (1848–1936), on the orders of the owner António August Carvalho Monteiro (1848–1920), it is a

Eating and Staying in Sintra

Lodging: Hotel Tivoli Palácio de Seteais is a luxury former palace just past the Regaleira Gardens on the outskirts of Sintra. (Rua Barbosa de Bocage; ☎ 21-923-3200; www.tivolihotels.com; doubles 125€–160€; AE, DC, MC, V. **Hotel Tivoli Sintra** (Praça da República; ☎ 21-923-7200; www.tivolihotels.com; doubles 80€–100€) is a lackluster block of a hotel with a dated interior but it's comfortable enough and located right in the heart of the town. **Penha Longa Golf & Hotel Resort** (Estrada da Lagoa Azul; ☎ 21-924-9011; www.penhalonga.com; doubles 175€–300€) is a large golf resort in the Sintra hills.

Dining: Cozinha Velha (€17–€22) is a renowned traditional restaurant in the former kitchens of the Palácio Nacional de Queluz (Largo do Palácio Nacional de Queluz; ☎ 21-435-6158). **Pateo de Garrett** (€10–€15) is an elegant restaurant in the heart of the town with Portuguese and international cuisine (Praça da República, 32; ☎ 21-923-2375).

The 18th-century Palacio Nacional de Queluz.

labyrinth of pathways leading past mythological characters, niches and watery grottoes, a chapel filled with erroneously mixed symbols of masonry and the Order of Christ, and a small neo-classical house. The idea was to create a mixture of universal and Portuguese mythical traditions, so you'll have to work hard to separate fact and fantasy. *Rua Barbosa de Bocage.* ☎ *21-910-6650. Admission 5€; 3.50€ 14–25 years and seniors. Open Mar & Oct daily 10am–6.30pm; Apr–Sep 10am–8pm; Nov–Jan 10am–5.30pm.*

⑤ Museu do Brinquedo. Sintra's Toy Museum is a treasure trove of toys from the past. One for the big kids, and you'll take a trip back to your youth and beyond with everything here from old tin cars and porcelain dolls to clockwork trains and Dinky toys. *Rua Visconde de Monserrate, 28* ☎ *21-924-2171. www.museu-do-brinquedo.pt. Admission 4€. Tue–Sun 10am–6pm.*

⑥ ★ Museu de Arte Moderno. This palatial building hosts temporary exhibitions by

internationally renowned artists focusing on movements such as Surrealism, Abstraction, Minimalism, Pop Art and Photography in the 90s. It has also worked for a long time with the Berardo Foundation, which has its outstanding Art Deco collection on display here. *Avenida Heliodoro Salgado* ☎ *21-924-8170. Admission 3€ Open Tues–Sun 10am–6pm.*

⑦ ★ Palacio Nacional de Queluz. This 18th-century pink palace, located between Lisbon and Sintra has rooms of period furniture, detailed cornices and heavy chandeliers, but for me the formal gardens outside are the main delight with their trimmed hedges and elaborate baroque fountains. The restaurant in the former royal kitchens is one of the best for Portuguese dining in the Lisbon area and known as the Cozinha Velha. *Largo do Palácio de Queluz,* ☎ *21-434-3860. Admission: 4€; 2€ 15–25 years and seniors; 1.6€ youth card holders; free under 14 years and Sun until 2pm. Open May–Sep daily 10am–6pm; Oct–Apr daily 10am–5pm.* ●

The
Savvy Traveler

Before You Go

ICEP Portugal—Portuguese Trade and Tourism Office
In the U.S. 590 Fifth Ave., New York, NY 10036 (☎ 646-723-0200); San Francisco (☎ 415-391-7080). **In Canada** 60 Bloor St. W., Suite 1005, Toronto, Ontario M4W 3B8 (☎ 416-921-7376). **In the U.K.** 3rd Floor, 11 Belgrave Sq., London SW1X 8PP (☎ 0845-355-1212).

The Best Time to Go

The Portuguese have their summer vacation from June till September and many *Lisboetas* leave the city at this time. It's not necessarily the heat they're escaping, as Lisbon's position at the mouth of the River Tagus means it's relieved by an Atlantic breeze. However, many take their summer break after Lisbon's festivities, which spread throughout June but dominate the first two weeks. The festivities also attract visitors in their hoards, so make sure you reserve your hotel well ahead if coming at this time. Afterwards, the locals are ready for a rest but the city continues to fill with tourists, mostly Europeans who have their summer holidays at this time. **March to May** and **September to late October** are quieter and the weather is still warm. From **November** to **February** you'll find Lisbon emptier, you can wander round the attractions without being bumped from pillar to post, and many of the hotels offer good deals. Over **New Year,** Lisbon fills again for *Reveillon* festivities, so reservations are essential.

Lisbon has become a popular city-break destination in the past few years, as well as hosting large conferences and events at the Feira Internacional de Lisbon (FIL) in Parque das Nações, and at some of the large business hotels with conference facilities. Therefore it's always advisable to reserve ahead to guarantee the hotel and better rates.

Festivals & Special Events

For information and updates on festivals, see www.visitlisboa.com, www.cm-lisboa.com/turismo, or www.whatsonwhen.com.

SPRING During March, the half marathon starts on the 25 de Abril Bridge, runs up river to Santa Apolónia Station, and back down to Belém. The Centro Cultural de Belém also holds its Spring Festival of classical music and crafts that month. During May, annual music festival **Superbock Superock** (www.superbock.pt/EN/sbsr.asp) takes over Tejo Park (Parque das Nações) for two weekends, attracting top bands from Portugal and overseas. Tennis fans will probably prefer to head to the Estádio Nacional for the **Estoril Open Tennis Championships** (www.estoril open.net), but tickets are hot property so you might only be able to see the qualifying rounds. At the end of May or beginning of June (depending on when Easter is), Roman Catholics celebrate **Corpus Christi**. There's a solemn parade of priests, religious orders, and the devoted from the Sé (cathedral) in the Alfama through the Baixa. The Holy Sacrament is held by the bishop under a canopy and given an armed guard. You'll see the devotion on some people's face at the sight of it, with tears streaming down their cheeks.

SUMMER Everything festival-wise in Lisbon builds up to the **Festas de Lisboa** in June. The main focus is on the city's patron, **St. Anthony,**

Useful Websites

www.visitportugal.com: Turismo de Portugal's official website; it has information on destinations and getting there, plus worldwide contacts.

www.portugaloffice.co.uk: The Portuguese National Tourist Office's official UK website divided into region and holiday type.

www.portugalvirtual.pt: Useful directory with guides, travel information, and tips.

www.cp.pt: The official Portuguese rail website, including schedule and route information, plus online booking.

www.atl-turismolisboa.pt: Lisbon's official tourism website with information on attractions, entertainment, tours, transport, accommodation, and restaurants in various languages.

www.estorilcoast.com: Official information on the Estoril coast, including Cascais and Sintra.

---

whose saint's day falls on June 13. The main event takes place the night before, starting with the *Casamentos* or marriages of 12 couples from different parishes in Lisbon; they drive through the Baixa to the Sé in vintage cars. Later in the evening, the *Marchas Populares* take place, featuring local and international groups performing traditional dances, theatrical performances, and folkloric reenactments along the Avenida da Liberdade. Seating is constructed along the pavement but these are mainly ticketed or reserved for important guests and the press. If you don't fancy squeezing in between for a peek, you can watch it on television at your hotel. Afterwards, crowds pour into the Alfama for a concert at the Castelo de São Jorge followed by all-night street parties. Temporary bars are set up in the street and on squares for a month of parties but this is the main night. It's definitely worth battling the crowds. Just watch your wallet and enjoy a plate of sardines and a glass of red wine or sangria, the typical dish and tipple of the night.

The rest of the summer is dominated by music festivals, including the **Sintra Festival of Music and Dance**, the **Estoril Jazz Festival**, and the **Cascais Summer Festival**. In Lisbon itself, the Calouste Gulbenkian Foundation hosts **Jazz em Agosto** (www.musica.gulbenkian.pt/jazz) and the **Superliga** soccer season (www.lpfp.pt) starts, giving you an opportunity to see Benfica and Sporting Portugal in action.

FALL   After a hot summer of festivals and music, things get back to business in October with **Moda Lisboa** (www.modalisboa.com), the Portuguese fashion industry's main event, attracting designers and models from around the world. In November, it's the turn of contemporary artists, who come for **Arte Lisboa** (www.artelisboa.fil.pt) at FIL in Parque das Nações.

WINTER   Like its neighbor, Spain, Portugal celebrates **All Saints' Day**

(November 1) as a public holiday, a time for remembering relatives and friends who have passed. The cemeteries become a glow of candles as visits are made to place flowers on graves.

To mark the end of the year, Lisbon hosts its own **Reveillon** party at the Torre de Belém. Stages are erected and international musicians invited to play. The concert is free and rounds off with a firework display, but the parties continue through the night in the Bairro Alto.

The winter comes to an end with **Carnaval**, in February, when there's a colorful Brazilian-style parade through the Bairro Alto and plenty of parties late into the night.

The Weather

Lisbon's southerly location means it has a Mediterranean feel, staying pretty warm throughout the year and never extremely cold in winter. Being located at the mouth of the River Tagus, there's an Atlantic breeze relieving the summer heat. During fall and winter the temperature averages around 17.1°C (62.8°F) and the sea is only a couple of degrees cooler than that. There are some beautiful blue-sky days and sometimes you won't even need a jacket, but the city isn't without its rain, so it's always advisable to take a raincoat. By mid-spring, temperatures have risen to an average of 21.8° C (71.2°F) making it pleasant enough to venture along the coast to the beach, and throughout the summer you can expect it to average around 26.3°C (79.3°F)—so take a hat, sunglasses, and plenty of sun cream.

Cellphones (Móviles)

World phones—or GSM (Global System for Mobiles) —work in Portugal (and most of the world). If your cellphone is on a GSM system, and you have a world-capable multiband phone, you can make and receive calls from Portugal. Just call your wireless operator and ask for "international roaming" to be activated. You can also rent a GSM phone. The French-owned store **FNAC** (main branch at Armázens do Chiado, Rua do Carmo, 2; metro: Baixa-Chiado; ☎ 707-313-435; www.fnac.pt) provides a pay-as-you-go mobile phone package, which could actually be cheaper than renting if you're staying just a few weeks or less. North Americans can rent a GSM phone before leaving home from **InTouch USA** (☎ 800-872-7626; www.intouchglobal.com) or **RoadPost** (☎ 888-290-1616; www.roadpost.com).

Car Rentals

With so many hills and narrow streets, driving in Lisbon's historic city center is not the most advisable form of transport and relatively few of the hotels here have parking facilities. More hotels in the financial and business district have parking but it's still very busy here. However, there are several arterial routes running through Lisbon and out of town, so a car is useful if you're going to explore the Estoril coast or further afield. Remember to take change with you as the motorways charge a toll. Several car hire companies operate from Lisbon's Portela Airport, including **Avis** (☎ 21-843-5550), **Budget** (☎ 21-994-2402), **Europcar** (☎ 21-840-1176), **Hertz** (☎ 21-843-8660), **Nacional/Alamo** (☎21-848-6191), and the lesser-known **Auto Jardim** (☎ 21-846-2916) and **Sixt** (☎ 21-847-0661). Most companies can also arrange pick-up at downtown offices or in Cascais and Estoril.

Getting **There**

By Plane

From Lisbon's **Portela** airport (12km/7 miles from the city center), there are several ways to get into town. One is the **Aerobus** Carris service (3.10€ one-day ticket or 1.20€ single from the bus driver, 2€ TAP ticket), which leaves from outside the arrivals terminal and stops at Marquês Pombal, Avenida de Liberdade, Restauradores, Rossio and Praça do Comércio. It operates daily between 7.45am and 8.45pm, departing every 20 minutes and taking approximately 30 minutes. The local bus service no. 44 travels to Parque das Nações, and there's a shuttle service running to Cascais/Estoril (8.50€).

There is also a **taxi** service operating from the airport. You'll need to pick up a Taxi Voucher from the Tourist Information stand in arrivals. Fares cost around 10€ but this is can go up if traffic is heavy. Remember to add 20% for weekends and between the hours of 9pm and 6am.

By Car

The **A1** *auto-estrada* or motorway leads to Lisbon from Porto. The **A2**

leads to the city from the Algarve, accessible via either the 25 de Abril Bridge downtown or the Vasco da Gama bridge in Parque das Nações. The **A5** runs from the Estoril coast area straight into the city center at Campolide and the **N19** runs between Portela Airport and Sintra. The **A6** links Spain at Badajoz to the **A2** just south of the city, and the **A25** from Salamanca in Spain links with the **A23** then **A1** north of Lisbon. Once you arrive at the city look out for signs to places downtown, including Pombal, Restauradores and Cais do Sodré, or Parque das Nações and Belém along the river.

By Train

Most long-distance national (Comboios de Portugal; www.cp.pt) and international trains from France and Spain arrive at **Oriente** (Parque das Nações) and **Santa Apolónia** (Avenida Infante Dom Henrique; ☎ 808-208-208 (info line); bus: 6, 12, 34). Trains from Estoril and Cascais run along the coast via Belém and terminate at **Cais do Sodré**, and trains from Sintra come into **Entrecampos**.

Getting **Around**

By Metro

The **Metropolitano de Lisboa**—usually known as the Metro (☎ 21-350-0115; www.metrolisboa.pt)—is Lisbon's clean and modern subway, and some of its stations are considered works of art as they're covered in Portugal's trademark tiles. The network doesn't cover the whole city but, for the areas where it does run, it's the quickest and easiest way to get around.

Single fares cost 0.75€ for 1 zone or 1.05€ for 2 zones. Return fares cost 1.35€ for 1 zone, 1.90€ for 2 zones. One-day tickets covering the metro and Carris (bus/tram and lifts, see below) cost 3.35€ or 13.50€ for 5 days. If you're staying longer than a few days, you can purchase a 7 Colinas card, which is a plastic card with a chip that can be topped up with credit at any metro station. All tickets must be validated at the entrance barriers before you board a train.

By Taxi

Cream taxis (older ones are black with a turquoise roof) are plentiful and reasonably priced. You can either hail a taxi in the street (the light on the roof means it's available) or grab one when they're lined up (at major squares, such as Rossio and Restauradores). Fares begin at 2.35€ (2.50 € at night). Reliable taxi companies include **Autocoope** (☎ 21-799-6460), **Rádio Taxis** (☎ 21-811-9000), and **Teletáxis** (☎ 21-811-1100). **Tips** are not expected.

By Bus

Buses are operated by Carris, run regularly and go to more places than the metro. However, if it's a choice between the two, the metro is a better option. Most bus routes make their way to the city center to Pombal, Avenida, Restauradores, Praça do Comércio, and Cais do Sodré. There's also a large bus station at Oriente. Carris also operates a night-bus service on eight routes from 11.45pm to 5.30am. Buy your ticket on board or validate your existing one by slotting it into the machine as you board the bus (by the driver).

By Car

Driving through the historic downtown will just frustrate you with its one-way systems, narrow, cobbled streets and hills, as well as lines of traffic and little parking. Even day trips to Sintra, Estoril, and Cascais are less stressful by train. However, if you plan on exploring the Estoril coast, the Sintra Natural Park or south to the Costa da Caparica, then a car is advisable, although the bus network is quite good.

On Foot

Lisbon's city center is best explored on foot but being built on seven hills this is only for fitter travelers. The Baixa is easy as it's flat and even all the way up the Avenida da Liberdade, but you might prefer to take a tram or funicular up to the Alfama, Chiado and Bairro Alto, and then walk downhill (note the Gloria funicular was closed for repairs at the time of writing). Belém is flat and pleasant where you can walk through parks and along the riverfront, but building work may mean walking along the busy Avenida da Brasília. The Parque das Nações is also pleasant to walk around as it's mainly pedestrianized, but again you can combine it with the cable car, tourist train, and cycle hire.

Fast **Facts**

Apartment Rentals Lisbon rental options include: **LisbonNet** (☎ 917-711-658; wwwlisbonet. com), which has apartments in the Bairro Alto; **www.holiday-lettings. com/lisbon**, with everything from basic apartments to luxury houses available for short-term lets in the city center and environs; and **onlyapartments** (www.only-apartments.com), which offers rentals for longer periods throughout the city center.

ATMs/Cashpoints Maestro, Cirrus, and Visa cards are readily accepted at all ATMs. Exchange currency either at banks, automatic currency exchange machines, or casas de câmbio (bureaux de change). There are currency exchange offices in both arrivals and departures at Portela Airport. Portuguese banks include the Banco de Portugal, Banco Espírito Santo e Comercial (BES), Banif, BPI, Credito Agricola, and Millennium

BCP. There are branches with ATMs throughout the city center, particularly in the Chiado, Baixa, Avenida da Liberdade, Saldanha, and Amoreiras. You'll also find ATMs in all the shopping centers.

Business Hours Banks are open Monday through Friday from 8:30am to 3pm. Most offices are open Monday through Friday from 9am to 6 or 7pm. At restaurants, lunch is usually from 12pm or 12.30pm to 2pm or 2.30pm and dinner from 7.30pm or 8pm to 10.30pm or 11pm. Shops generally open Monday to Friday 9am or 10am and close at 7pm. Some close from 1–3pm during the week and in the Chiado/Baixa some stay open till 8pm or 9pm. Major shopping centers stay open until midnight every day.

Consulates and Embassies
U.S. Embassy, Avenida das Forças Armadas (☎ 21-727-3300); **Canadian Embassy**, Avenida da Liberdade, 196-200, 3rd floor (☎ 21-314-8054); **U.K. Embassy**, Rua de São Bernardo, 33 (☎ 21-392-4000); **Australian Embassy**, Avenida Liberdade, 196-200, 2nd floor (☎ 21-310-1500); **New Zealand Consulate**, Rua do Periquito, Lote A-13, Quinta da Bicuda, Cascais (☎ 21-370-5779). **South African Embassy**, Avenida Luís Bívar, 10 (☎ 21-355-5931).

Doctors Dial ☎ 112 in an emergency.

Electricity Most hotels operate on 220/380 volts AC (50 hertz). Plugs are European Standard. To use an American-style plug, you'll need a 220-volt transformer and adapter plug.

Emergencies For an ambulance or medical emergencies, fire or police, call ☎ 112.

Gay and Lesbian Travelers In 1982, 7 years after the end of the Salazar dictatorship, Portugal decriminalized homosexuality in private among consenting adults. In 1995, it adjusted the law on crimes related to sexuality to reflect individual right to sexual freedom. Due to the strong influence of the Roman Catholic Church on Portuguese society, further legislation was slow to pass, but civil unions between same-sex couples were eventually legalized in 2001, and in 2004 the constitution banned discrimination on the basis of sexual orientation. At the time of writing the reality of this was still being fought in the courts by a lesbian couple who were refused a marriage license. Gay rights' groups are active in Portugal, the largest of which is ILGA-Portugal (www.ilga-portugal.oninet.pt), which have helped organize events such as Gay Pride and Gay and Lesbian Film Festivals. There are also various gay bars and clubs in Lisbon (see p 122).

Holidays Public holidays observed include: January 1 (New Year's Day), February (Mardi Gras/Carnival), March/April (Good Friday and Easter Monday), April 25 (Liberty Day—Carnation Revolution), May 1 (May Day), May (Corpus Christi), June 10 (National Day), June 13 (St. Anthony's Day), August 15 (Feast of the Assumption), October 5 (Republic Day), November 1 (All Saints' Day), December 1 (Restoration of Independence Day), December 8 (Feast of the Immaculate Conception), and December 25 (Christmas).

Insurance You should check any existing insurance policies, making sure you purchase any necessary additional travel insurance to cover cancellations, lost luggage, theft, medical expenses, and car rental insurance. For more information, contact one of the following insurers: **Access America** (☎ 800-284-8300; www.accessamerica.com); **Travel Guard International** (☎ 800-826-4919; www.travelguard.com);

Travel Insured International (☎ 800-243-3174; www.travel insured.com); and **Travelex Insurance Services** (☎ 800-228-9792; www.travelex-insurance.com). For travel overseas, most U.S. health plans (including Medicare and Medicaid) do not provide coverage, and the ones that do often require payment for services upfront. If you require additional medical insurance, try **MEDEX Assistance** (☎ 800-537-2029; www.medexassist.com) or **Travel Assistance International** (☎ 800-821-2828; www.travel assistance.com).

Internet Internet access is becoming easy to find, from hotel lobbies (which regularly offer Wi-Fi) to cybercafés (*cafés Internet*). There are also a lot of internet cafés and access points. **Lisbon Welcome Center** in Praça de Comércio has several terminals. Other places include Cyber.Bica at Rua dos Duques de Bragança, 7, www.cyber bica.com; Ciber Chiado, Largo do Picadeiro, 10; Net Lisboa Café, Rua Padre Francisco, 24 C. Webc@fe, Rua Diário de Noticias, 126; Cib@r Café, Pavilhão de Conhecimento.

Lost Property You should call credit card companies as soon as you discover your wallet has been lost or stolen and file a report at the nearest police station. Your credit card company may require a police report number or record. **American Express** cardholders and travelers' check holders should call ☎ 800-869-3016 in the U.S., or ☎ 21-427-0400 in Portugal. **Diners Club** U.S. emergency number is ☎ 300-792-0629, or ☎ 21-315-9856 in Portugal. **MasterCard** holders should call ☎ 636-722-7111 in the U.S., or ☎ 800-811-272 in Portugal. **Visa** U.S. emergency number is ☎ 800-847-2911, or ☎ 800-811-824 in Portugal.

Mail & Postage Portuguese post offices are called *correios* (koh-ray-os), identified by red signs with a white logo depicting a man on a horse playing a bugle and the word *Correios* below. Main offices are generally open from Mon–Fri 9am–6pm, but the main post office in Praça dos Restauradores (☎ 21-323-8971) is open Mon–Fri 8am–10pm, Sat and Sun 9am–6pm. Other branches are at the Centro Cultural de Belém (Praça do Império), Campo Pequeno (Rua Arco do Cego, 88), and the airport (24-hour service).

Money The single European currency in Portugal is the **euro** (€), divided into 100 cents. At press time, the exchange rate was approximately €1 = \$1.41 or £0.70. For up-to-the-minute exchange rates between the euro and the dollar, check the currency converter website **www.xe.com**.

Passports U.S., Canadian, Australian, and New Zealand visitors to Portugal do not need a visa if their stay does not exceed 90 days. South African visitors do need a visa. If your passport is lost or stolen, contact your country's embassy or consulate immediately. See "Consulates & Embassies" above. You should make a copy of your passport's critical pages and keep it separate from the original.

Pharmacies Pharmacies *(farmacias)* operate from Mon–Fri 9am–1pm and 3–7pm and Saturday mornings. There are also 24-hour pharmacies, which follow a schedule displayed in the window. To find a pharmacy near you, call ☎ 800-202-134.

Police The national police emergency number is ☎ 112. For local police, call ☎ 21-321-7000.

Safety Lisbon doesn't have a high violent crime rate compared to many other cities, but there has been a rise in incidents in the past couple of decades. It's generally safe to walk around Lisbon even at night but you should be cautious in parts of the Alfama and Bairro Alto, particularly narrow streets where it's quieter and not so well lit. Just don't walk alone or take a taxi back to your hotel. Most establishments will be happy to call one for you. Also watch your belongings on Tram 28, which is renowned for pickpockets. Almost everyday someone loses something because they're too busy looking out of the window. You don't have to miss out on the attractions. Just hold onto your wallet and watch, or put your bag at the front where you can see it, and you shouldn't have a problem.

If you are unlucky enough to be a victim of crime, there's a dedicated Tourism Police office at Palácio Foz (the same building as the Tourist Office) in Praça dos Restauradores (☎ 21-342-634).

Smoking   On January 1, 2008, Portugal introduced a smoking ban in enclosed spaces in public places and commercial establishments. However, proprietors of spaces larger than 100m^2 can choose to allow or prohibit smoking, but they must make display signs and provide designated smoking areas. ANA, the Portuguese aiport authority followed by announcing a full ban on smoking in public areas (from February 2008) at all airports except Lisbon, where there are designated smoking areas.

Taxes   The value-added (VAT) tax (known in Portugal as *IVA*) ranges from 5% to 21%, depending on the commodity being sold. Food, wine, and basic necessities are taxed at 5%; most goods and services (including car rentals) at 12%; luxury items (jewelry, all tobacco, imported liquors) at 21%; and hotels at 5%. Non-EU residents are entitled to a reimbursement of the 21% IVA tax on most purchases worth more than 59.36€ made at shops offering "Tax

Free" or "Global Refund" shopping. You should ask the store for a declaration form when you purchase the item(s), detailing the amount paid, the amount bought ,and the amount to be reimbursed. You can claim the reimbursement at the airport in cash, by credit card or international check, but you must show the items in question to the Customs officials beforehand. For more information see www.premiertaxfree.com and www.portugaltaxrefund.com.pt.

Telephones   For national telephone information, dial ☎ 118. For international telephone information, dial ☎ 177. If you want to make an international call, dial ☎ 00 followed by the country code, area code, and number. If you're making a local or long-distance call in Portugal, dial the 2-digit city code first (**21** in the Lisbon area) followed by the 7-digit number. Public phones take coins or phonecards, which can be bought at the post office or *tabacaria* (newsagent) booths. You can also make calls from phone booths at post offices.

Tipping   Menu prices should usually include the 12% service charge. Leaving a tip is discretionary but in more expensive restaurants and tourist areas a tip of 5% to 10% is becoming more common. For coffees and snacks you don't need to tip, although some people leave a few small coins. Taxis do not expect tips but you should tip hotel porters, doormen, and maids 1€ per day.

Toilets   In Portugal they're called *casas de banho* or *lavabos,* and are labeled *homens* for men and *senhoras* for women.

Tourist Information   Lisbon Welcome Center, Praça de Comércio (☎ 21-031-2810), is open daily 9am to 8pm. There are other Turismo de Portugal offices or kiosks at **Palácio Foz**, Praça dos Restauradores (☎ 21-346-3314); **Aeroporto de Portela**, Arrivals Hall (☎ 21-845-660);

Estação de Santa Apolónia, International Terminal (☎ 21-882-1606); **Rua Augusta**, Baixa (☎ 21-325-9131); and by the **Mosteiro dos Jerónimos**, Belém (☎ 21-365-8435).

Tours. Cityline/Sightline (☎ 21-343-1405; www.cityline-sightline.pt) operates hop-on, hop-off bus tours around the city, with 13 stops close to major attractions. Tickets cost 15€ for 1 day and 22€ for 2-day tickets (children 7.50€ and 11€). Buses start at Praça de Pombal and also pass Rossio Square, Praça de Comércio, Cais do Sodré, and Belém.

They also operate out-of-town tours to the Estoril coast and Fatima.

Travelers with Disabilities Portugal has been coming in line with EU regulations and many modern hotels now have ramps and lifts, and there are also lifts at most main stations on the metro. There are disabled parking spaces and lifts at the airport, and assistance is also available, but you need to request this at the time of booking. **Accessible Portugal** (☎ 919-195-980; www.accessibleportugal.com) offers escorted tours, mainly operating out of Lisbon.

Lisbon: **A Brief History**

205 B.C. Romans form a municipality in Lisbon, naming it *Felicitus Julia*.

5TH–6TH C. A.D. German tribes occupy the city, including the Vandals and the Visigoths, calling it *Ulishbona*.

711 Moors (Muslims from north Africa) arrive on the Iberian peninsular, taking Lisbon (*Al-Ushbuna*) 3 years later, building a fortress on top of the Al-Hamma (Alfama).

1147 Dom Afonso Henriques takes the city, helped by crusaders, including the Order of Christ. He orders the building of the Sé (cathedral) on top of the mosque.

12TH–13TH C. Commercial links with north Africa improve and those in professions linked to navigation (carpenters and sailors) are given special privileges.

1256 Dom Afonso III moves his court to Lisbon and makes it the new capital of the country.

1290 Dom Dinis creates the first university in Lisbon but moves it to Coimbra in 1308.

1308 Portugal makes its first commercial treaty with England.

1383–5 Dom Fernando I dies without an heir, leaving way for João of Castille (Dom João I) to become king, but civil war and disease reign for two years.

1386 The Treaty of Windsor reinforces the Anglo–Portuguese alliance, along with the marriage between Dom João I and Philippa of Lancaster.

1415 The Infante Dom Henrique (Prince Henry the Navigator) conquers Ceuta, heralding the Golden Age of Discovery.

1487 Bartolomeu Dias rounds the Cape of Good Hope.

1498 Vasco da Gama reaches India, providing a new spice route and other commercial activity.

1500 Pedro Alvares Cabral arrives in Bahia (Brazil).

1501 Work begins on the Mosteiro dos Jerónimos, ordered by Dom Manuel I and in the Manueline style named after him.

1540 The first *auto da fé* takes place in Rossio Square, the public trial and massacre of people of Jewish heritage.

1572 Luis Vaz de Camões' epic poem of history and maritime discovery, *Os Lusadas* (The Lusiads), is first published.

1580 Two years after Dom Sebastião dies without an heir, Dom Felipe I (Felipe II of Spain) is crowned king.

1640 Following the War of Restoration, the Duque de Bragança (Dom João IV) takes the throne, and the old commercial alliance with England is reinstated.

17TH–18TH C. Gold discovered in Brazil is used to build luxurious palaces and convents.

1755 An earthquake and subsequent tsunami, fires and disease devastate Lisbon, killing around 10,000 people.

LATE 18TH C. Marquês de Pombal, Prime Minister to Dom José I, rebuilds the city, which brings new commercial activity.

1807 Napoleonic troops enter the city, but it is retaken a year later with the help of the English.

1822 Brazil wins independence and Dom Pedro I becomes the first emperor.

19TH C. Civil wars over accession to the throne.

1836 The old Inquisition House in Rossio is demolished, due to campaigning by writer Almeida Garrett, and the Teatro Dona Maria II is built in its place.

1856–70 First railway line is built between Lisbon and Carregado, followed by lines to Porto and the building of Santa Apolónia and Rossio stations.

1878 Electricity comes to Lisbon and the first lifts up the hills are installed around 1880.

1886 Avenida da Liberdade is constructed.

1910 Revolution and declaration of the First Republic.

1914–17 Portugal joins the allies during the First World War.

1918 Spanish flu kills thousands.

1926–33 First Republic ends and a military dictatorship rules.

1933–74 Semi-fascist *Novo Estado* (New State) imposed by António de Oliveira de Salazar.

1935 Writer Fernando Pessoa dies of a hepatic ulcer.

1960 Padrão dos Descobrimentos rebuilt to commemorate the 500th anniversary of the death of Henry the Navigator.

1966 Ponte Salazar, a bridge across the Tagus River, is inaugurated, later renamed Ponte 25 de Abril.

1974 On April 25, the peaceful Carnation Revolution takes power.

1975 First democratic elections in 50 years won by the Social Democrat Party.

1986 Portugal joins the E.U.

1992 The Centro Cultural de Belém is inaugurated.

1994 Lisbon is European Capital of Culture, attracting visitors and international attention.

1998 Lisbon hosts Expo '98 in the newly built Parque das Nações.

2004 Portugal hosts the European soccer championships, with the final taking place at Lisbon's Estádio da Luz.

Useful Phrases

Useful Words & Phrases

ENGLISH	PORTUGUESE	PRONUNCIATION
Good day	Bom día	*bom-dee-ah*
How are you?	Como está?	*kohm shtah*
Very well	Muito bem	*moy-to bey-m*
Thank you	Obrigado/a	*o-bree-gah-doh /dah*
You're welcome	De nada	*deh nah-dah*
Goodbye	Adeus	*ah-day-oosh*
Please	Por favor/Faz favor	*por fah-vohr/fash fah-voh*
Yes	Sim	*si-(m)*
No	Não	*now*
Excuse me	Desculpe	*deh-shkoolp*
Where is . . . ?	Onde fica ...?	*ohn-day fee-kah...?*
To the right	À direito	*ah deer-eh-toh*
To the left	À esquerda	*ah esh-kair-dah*
I would like . . .	Eu gostaria...	*eh-ooh gosh-tah-ree-ya*
I want . . .	Quero...	*kair-roh...*
Do you have . . . ?	Tem?	*Tay-m?*
How much is it?	Quanto é?/	*kwahn-toh eh?/*
	Quanto custa?	*kwahn-toh coosh-tah?*
When?	Quando?	*kwahn-doh?*
What?	Como? / O qué?	*Coh-moh? / oh-keh?*
There is (Is there . . . ?)	Ha . . . ?	*aye/ee ah/ee ahn*
Yesterday	Ontem	*ohn-tey-m*
Today	Hoje	*ohj*
Tomorrow	Amanha	*ah-mah-nyah-ah*
Good	Bom	*boh-m*
Bad	Mau	*m-owh*
Better (Best)	(O) melhor	*(oh) meh-ly-ohr*
More	Mais	*my-sh*
Less	Menos	*meh-nohs/meh-nyus*
Do you speak English?	Fala inglês?	*Fah-lah eeng-gleysh?*
I speak a	Falo um pouco	*Fah-loh oom poh-koh*
little Portuguese	de português	*day port-you-qeysh*
I don't understand	Não percebo	*now pair-seb-oh*
What time is it?	Qué horas são?	*keh oh-rahsh s-owh*
The check, please	À conta, faz favor	*ah con-tah fash fah-vohr*
The station	À estação	*ah es-tah-saoh*
a hotel	um hotel	*oom oh-tehl*
the market	o mercado	*oh mehr-kah-doh*
restaurant	um restaurante	*oom rehs-tow-rahnt*
the toilet	o lavabo	*oh lah-vah-boh*
a doctor	um médico	*oon meh-dee-koh*
the road to . . .	a estrada	*ah esh-trah-dah*
to eat	comer	*ko-mehr*
a room	um cuarto	*oom quah-toh*
a book	um livro	*oom lee-vroh*
a dictionary	um diccionario	*oom dik-syoh-nah-ryoh*

Numbers

NUMBER	PORTUGUESE	PRONUNCIATION
1	um	*oom*
2	dois	*doysh*
3	três	*tresh*
4	cuatro	*kwah-troh*
5	cinco	*sink-oh*
6	seis	*saysh*
7	sete	*set*
8	oito	*oy-toh*
9	nove	*nov*
10	dez	*desh*
11	onze	*onz*
12	doze	*doz*
13	treze	*treh-z*
14	catorze	*kah-tohr-z*
15	quinze	*kin-z*
16	dezaseis	*dez-ah-saysh*
17	dezasete	*dez-ah-set*
18	dezoito	*dez-oy-to*
19	dezanove	*dez-ah-nov*
20	vinte	*vint*
30	trinta	*trin-tah*
40	quarenta	*kwah-rehn-tah*
50	cinquenta	*sing-kwehn-tah*
60	sessenta	*seh-sehn-tah*
70	setenta	*seh-tehn-tah*
80	oitenta	*oy-tehn-tah*
90	noventa	*noh-behn-tah*
100	cem	*cey-m*

Glossary

avenida avenue
azulejos tiles
capela chapel
casa house
castelo castle
fado a type of melancholy Portuguese folk song
igreja church
jardim garden
miradouro viewpoint
mosteiro monastery
museu museum
parque park
praça square
rio river
rua street
sé cathedral
teatro theater
torre tower

Index

Photo **Credits**

Explore over 3,500 destinations.

TOKYO — 7766 miles
LONDON — 3818 miles
TORONTO — 4682 miles
SYDNEY — 5087 miles
NEW YORK — 4947 miles
LOS ANGELES — 2556 miles
HONG KONG — 5638 miles

Frommers.com makes it easy.

Find a destination. ✓ Book a trip. ✓ Get hot travel deals.
Buy a guidebook. ✓ Enter to win vacations. ✓ Listen to podcasts.
Check out the latest travel news. ✓ Share trip photos and memories.
And much more.

Frommers.com

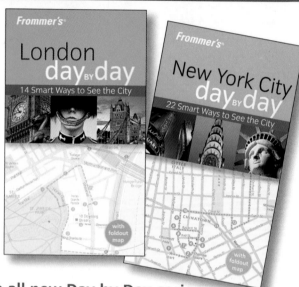